I0449747

YOU CAN BE RICH TOO

(HOW TO BREAK FREE FROM THE SHACKLES OF POVERTY)

Philip U. Nkwocha

authorHOUSE®

AuthorHouse™ UK Ltd.
500 Avebury Boulevard
Central Milton Keynes, MK9 2BE
www.authorhouse.co.uk
Phone: 08001974150

© 2010 Philip U. Nkwocha. All rights reserved.

No part of this book may be reproduced, stored in a retrieval system, or transmitted by any means without the written permission of the author.

First published by AuthorHouse   9/17/2010

ISBN: 978-1-4520-6431-4 (e)
ISBN: 978-1-4520-6430-7 (sc)

For further information or permission address to:

AuthorHouse UK LTD
Email: philipnkwocha@rocketmail.com

This book is printed on acid-free paper.

To all who recognize God as their source and believe Him in their journey out of the shackles of poverty to prosperity.

To my lovely wife, Blessing.

Contents

Foreword

Man is created for increase, advancement and prosperity. This concept has eluded and made many to be at a standstill for donkey years. Philip Nkwocha in this book explains that from conception, birth, growth and development of man are lessons from nature that man is destined to prosper.

Prosperity in some Christian cycles is a new doctrine that is gaining ground very much in this generation. This is because of the previous mindset of these people concerning prosperity. From origin God determines that man prospers. That is why in 3 John 2, the Scriptures state that we may prosper and be in health even as our soul prospers. God is interested in three dimensional prosperity of man – physical, spiritual and material prosperity. It is imperative that the physical and material prosperity go along side with the prosperity of the soul.

Abraham served God and he prospered. Other Patriarchs also are clear examples of those whom God rewarded with riches. These are perfect examples for us to follow.

Poverty is not synonymous with spirituality. One may be poor and is far from God. At the same time, one may be rich and sets not his heart on those riches and is very close to God.

Poverty is in the mind and wealth is in the mind. The ability to harness this great potential deposited in man is what makes the difference.

In this book, the author explains why you should prosper, highlights the reproaches of poverty and emphasizes the need for a mental reorientation. He opined that you can secure your future through development of financial intelligence. According to him, when all these things are properly put in place, you will find yourself on the better side of life.

It is my opinion that this is a must read book. It is a book that revolutionizes the mind and opens our eyes to our past mistakes. It will take us to the road of financial freedom.

Happy reading!

Rev. S. I. Brodrick
Assistant District Superintendent
Assemblies of God
Apapa District, Lagos, Nigeria

Introduction

Despite unsavoury little beginning and seemingly protracted battle with poverty you can rise above the ashes of defeat and primordial enslaving sentiments associated with it. You don't need to be held down by your present poor state any more. The battle against poverty is the battle you can and should win. And the time to act is now. In confronting poverty there are techniques that are effective and there are impotent ones. Mourning, murmuring, complaining, procrastination, self pontification, playing blame game, etc, cannot solve the poverty problems. People that depend on these to solve the poverty problem only end up in deeper pains and losses. But those that discover and apply Godly financial principles as enunciated in this book gain freedom from misery of poverty to abundant riches.

Poverty scourge can be overcome. I have had my tango with poverty and I can boldly testify that the battle against poverty can be won. I had a poor background and really it wasn't funny or easy but I have overcome the battle against poverty and I am on the path of incremental riches with godliness and contentment.

Riches are not the sole preserve of any one. Don't be fooled to believe that anyone has exclusive rights to riches. That you are poor today does not mean that you can't be rich tomorrow if you consistently learn and do the right things that lead to increase. This is the essence of this book. You have your portion of the Earth's enormous resources. You can move from poverty to riches. This is possible! But riches will not come to you by mere wishes. You've got to work for this and now is the time.

As righteousness is better than wickedness and light is better than darkness so are riches better than poverty. Transiting from the ashes of poverty to beauty of riches is possible. Many have defied odds against them and have through application of financial principles walked way from the reproaches of poverty and are enjoying the wondrous and abundant provisions of God. You can do this too. You can live a full and prosperous life.

God above all wants you to prosper materially and be in health even as your soul prospers. To set you on this pedestal Jesus was crucified on the cross at Calvary to redeem you from Satan, sin, sickness, poverty and death. The price of poverty was paid by Jesus Christ over two thousand years ago. Carrying the excess baggage of poverty is destructive and not helpful. Drop it now!

Poverty is never the best for you. It was not there from the beginning. It came in as part consequence of the fall of man. Poverty is not piety. Living in abject poverty with fallacious assumption that this is pleasing to God is the worst deceit that anyone can be saddled with.

In Chapter One, twenty one reasons are adduced on why you should prosper. God's first command to you is to prosper. Prosperity is a covenant birthright for those that serve and obey God. The teachings of Jesus on money making and management are elaborately enunciated in Chapter Two. Chapter three dwells extensively on the comparative life styles of Abraham and Lazarus. Both feared God and served Him while here on earth but believed God differently when it comes to prosperity matters. While Abraham flourished on all sides of life, Lazarus lived beggarly and the question is, why believe like Abraham and live like Lazarus?

The reproaches of poverty and the story of my transition from poverty to riches come to the fore on Chapters Four and Five respectively. That you can overcome poverty without cutting corners is the astonishing and reassuring truth that is alive in this book through my journey from wretchedness to happiness and riches. You are what you think. To overcome poverty the journey must commence with mental reorientation. If you are poor on the inside you will obviously be poor on the outside. Conversely if you are rich in your thoughts this will reflect on the results obtained. This is the focus of Chapter Six.

In Chapter Seven the urgent needs to create multiple streams of income are highlighted. Today's economic realities are evident that one source of income may not be enough to sustain a comfortable lifestyle. Thus it is incumbent on you to listen and obey age long Biblical teachings on Multiple Streams of Income.

Wishes alone cannot take you out of poverty. You can and should develop financial intelligence. Money can be grown. Chapter Eight teaches you how to do this.

Chapter Nine urges you to come to the better side of life. You can do it and now is the time.

Have a good reading.

ACKNOWLEDGMENT

I want to thank the Almighty God for the inspiration and grace given to me to put this book together.

My undiminished love goes to my wife for her support and understanding during the times and seasons when I was writing this book. Her contributions and critiques helped in making this book worth while. I will not fail to mention the many times she slept on the couch while I was on the reading table writing.

To the kids, Chukwuemeka, Ugonma, and Chimzurum, I appreciate their fond disturbances, their running around and inquisitiveness into what dad was writing and their often toying both with the computer and manuscripts of this book are all commendable and contributed in no small measure to this great work.

To my local church pastors, Reverend Titus C. Ibekwe, Basil Ugwu and Godwin Ude and my fellow deacons I want to say I am sincerely grateful for all their support and opportunities given to me to minister in the church. The brethren in Assemblies of God, Agboju, Lagos, Nigeria aka Agape Love Family are all wonderful.

I wish to acknowledge the Assistant District Superintendent of Assemblies of God, Apapa, Lagos, Nigeria Reverend S. I. Brodrick who wrote the preface of this book. I thank him very much for being a source of inspiration and a great blessing to the body of Christ. I will not fail to mention the contributions and prayers of the following trojans of faith, Reverend Voke Uchemu, Evangelist Daniel Ndubuisi, Pastors Ndubuisi Opara, Alex Nwachukwu, Florence Emenike, Chinaecheozor Ohaeri and God's Bulldozer, Evangelist Ben Nkwocha. You've been very supportive and may our good God richly bless you.

To my prayer partners and others too numerous to mention I wish to say I am sincerely appreciative.

Thanks to Mr. Kola Owolabi for editing this book. My partners in AuthorHouse UK especially Michael Shorey and Liam Brandom were impressive in counseling and publishing this book.

Chapter 1

WHY YOU SHOULD PROSPER

From the little seed in the womb to a full grown man; from the tiny mustard seed to the biggest herbs; from crèche to doctor of letters; from Stone Age to Information Age, nature teaches us that man is made for growth, increase and prosperity. Just as every creature gives birth to its kind -lion to lion; sheep to sheep; goat to goat, human to human, etc, God births sons like Him.

Every purpose of God prospers. Every work of God also prospers. You are the hand work of God; you are good and should prosper. The word of God which accomplishes the purpose of God prospers and never comes back unfruitful. Because you are an offspring of the Almighty God you have the gene of prosperity in you and the word of God is coming to you through this book to prosper.

There are many Scriptural reasons you should be prosperous in every ramification of life. Sadly there are also many circumstantially compelling and possibly genuine reasons you should continue to be poor, wretched and frustrated. But the person you will ultimately become depends on what you make out of what God is saying about prosperity and what your circumstances are saying. If you align with God and obey Him you will obviously not fail because God does not fail. He's ever faithful and will bless all that respond obediently to His word. Unfortunately many believe the reports of man-made experts that destroy hope having no basis on the word of God. Juxtapose God's word with what others are saying. If they are not in sync with what God has said concerning you and any condition of life, then

1

know that these are junk and cannot be true and of help to you. Thus your best option is to throw such trash away and feel no harm.

There are so many reasons you should be poor but let's concentrate on why you should prosper:

1. God's first command to man is to prosper

God's word is eternally true, efficacious and cannot lose its power. What He said yesterday stands now and forever. In the very beginning, before the fall of man in the Garden of Eden, God's first instruction to him was to prosper. This instruction is true now as then. Its potency has not changed.

> *"God blessed them and said to them, "Be fruitful and increase in number; fill the earth and subdue it. Rule over the fish of the sea and the birds of the air and over every living creature that moves on the ground."(Genesis 1:28 NIV)*

Be fruitful means to be productive; to be rich; to be successful; to be fertile; to enlarge and have in abundance, etc. God's first order to man was not: "Thou shall have no other gods beside me......," as was detailed in the book of Exodus Chapter Twenty. This came after the fall. Even before the injunction to man in Genesis 2: 17 that says: *"you must not eat from the tree of the knowledge of good and evil, for when you eat of it you will surely die,"* God had expressly commanded man to be fruitful, to multiply, to replenish, to subdue, to dominate. ***The prosperous ones dominate; slackers don't ever exercise rule. Neither does financial slaves exact authority.***

Let me reiterate that before the giving of the Ten Commandments in Exodus Chapter 20, was this first command to man to prosper as stated in Genesis 1:28. The God of heaven and earth that commanded man to subdue the land, air and sea and access all the resources therein expects us to be fruitful in multiples in everything we do. This is His purpose but one can choose to ignore this and live wretched.

God is out to bless you. He will bless you as you exploit the earth through the works of your hands. ***He does not bless or multiply empty***

hands. Be engaged in genuine endeavors and trust God to bless the work of your hand. My authority in asserting that you were created to prosper is because God's first law to man was to be fruitful and keep multiplying. Adam before the fall never lacked. He was surrounded with precious gold and inexhaustible natural resources. All the animals, fishes and trees were at his command. But what man lost as a result of the fall in the Garden of Eden he stands to regain in Christ. In restored state in Christ you should not lack for the Lord is your Shepherd and you shall not want (Psalm 23:1).

2. Prosperity is a covenant right

God operates through covenants. The blood of Jesus Christ brings us into covenant relationship with God. We are Children of God and joint heirs with Christ. Every covenant has its conditions. It behooves on us once the covenant cord is struck with God to fulfill our side of the bargain in order to access all the promises contained in the covenant. God for sure is ever faithful to keep to His word. What God demands of us is willingness and obedience. This entails knowing what to do and taking action accordingly.

> *"If you are willing and obedient, you shall eat the good of the land."* *(Isaiah 1:19 NKJV)*

> *"If you fully obey the LORD your God and carefully follow all his commands I give you today, the LORD your God will set you high above all the nations on earth. All these blessings will come upon you and accompany you if you obey the LORD your God."* *(Deuteronomy 28:1-2 NIV)*

God's blessings will only overtake us when we are willing and obedient to His words. ***Obedience brings blessings.*** It is immaterial whether you are tall or short; black or white; had a good or bad start in life. Willingness and obedience is demanded by God and where these qualities are found God will prove faithful. Willingness has to do with your inward desire for change which is expressed in your outward obedience to God's word.

When Jesus died on the cross He crushed the forces of sin, poverty, sickness and death. The floodgates of heaven were opened to whosoever will through the Cross. Jesus has paid the price for poverty ushering us into the realm of abundance. This was part of the debt we could not pay. He substituted his riches for our poverty. This is true spiritually and financially. Thus there is no need any more to keep carrying the heavy and destructive load of poverty. Your poverty has been paid for. Why are you still carrying the heavy garbage of poverty? Do away with it now before it's too late.

> *"For you know the grace of our Lord Jesus Christ that though he was rich, yet for your sakes he became poor, so that you through his poverty might become rich."*

> 2 Corinthians 8:9 (NIV)

Undoubtedly from the Scripture quoted above the price of prosperity was paid by Jesus. For your sake He became poor that you might become rich. You don't need to be poor anymore. You may look at your purse and the millions of naira or dollars are not there yet. Wait they are coming. Your circumstances might be a stark contradiction to the fact that you are very rich. Don't give up! Keep moving ahead. You don't even need to feel that you are rich to know you are rich. This is immaterial because you are already rich. As far as God is concerned you are rich.

Becoming rich is a process or a journey which you must embrace or embark on to actualize this immutable truth. It does not matter what men, any global economic melt down, adversities and circumstances of life including your pocket are saying. Their opinion is inconsequential compared to God's opinion of your wellness. God said you are rich, do believe this and live by the knowing. And that settles it. Every action you are taking should be done with expectations of receiving the best because of your covenant position in God.

In 3 John 1-3, the Lord calls you to prosper in all things.

> *"Beloved, I pray that you may prosper in all things and be in health, just as your soul prospers." (NKJV)*

John talked about three dimensional prosperity – unbroken and working relationship with God, material prosperity and healthy living. This is the will of God concerning you. And you have got to step out in obedience to enjoy these covenant provisions.

3. The earth's resources belong to God and they are for our use

"*The earth is the Lord's, and everything in it, the world, and all who live in it*"

(Psalm 24:1 NIV)

The earth, the totality of its resources and the users of those resources belong to God whether they all realize this truth or not. All the precious jewels and cattle are His and He knows where they are. Thus we must depend on Him to lead us in the part of profit.

"*For every animal of the forest is mine, and the cattle on a thousand hills. I know every bird in the mountains, and the creatures of the field are mine.*"

(Psalm 50:10-11 NIV)

"*The silver is mine and the gold is mine,' declares the LORD Almighty.*"

(Haggai 2:8 NIV)

God did not put the solid and liquid minerals or natural resources in the land and seas for His use and benefit. *All the earth resources are not to build heavenly super structures. God for example will not come to use earthly gold to make the golden streets of heaven. Earth's best precious stones will be too inferior for such purpose.* The point here is that these resources are for our growth, development and enjoyment. Don't wait to go to heaven to drive the best cars this world can offer and you can afford. You will be disappointed not to find the Toyotas, Hondas, BMWs, Mercedes', Fords, Nissans, Hummer Jeeps, etc, of this world up there in heaven. What heaven holds is incomparable with these world inferior offerings which in our fickle minds are superlative. The mind cannot fathom what heaven has in stock waiting for us up there.

"The highest heavens belong to the LORD, but the earth he has given to man."

(Psalm 115:16 NIV)

The Lord unequivocally gave man this earth and we must dominate and enjoy it. Every one under the sun has a portion of what God has freely deposited in the earth. I have my own share of God's abundance of cattle, silver and gold and the best that God offers while we are here on earth. And so do you. Wake up to this reality and go for your own share of God's best. You are not there yet. Arise.

Often we dwell on the down side of the story of the prodigal son in Luke 15:12-31. How he was profligate, spoilt and sinful! But we fail to learn from his positive attributes. The older brother had all that belonged to the father but he never really enjoyed any. He was only filled with anger, resentment and bitterness. ***The prodigal son walked up to the father and requested for his own portion of inheritance and he got it.*** The father never rebuked nor scolded him for daring to ask but gladly gave him his due portion.

The older brother who by birth had the first right of inheritance was probably waiting for the death of the father before he could enter into his possession just as many are "waiting for the death of God" for His riches to become theirs. Please note that you will be highly disappointed if you are waiting for God to die for you to receive your inheritance from Him. God is preeminently eternal and cannot die. Jesus has died the death on our behalf over two thousand years ago. He will never die again. The price has been paid once and for all. Yours is to inherit what rightly belongs to you. That is why God in Romans 8:17 calls us joint heirs with Christ – joint inheritors of the wealth of God.

4. The profit sharing of the earth is for all

I work with an organization that shares a portion of each year's profit to the staff. The company recognizes the importance of making all that contributed to the baking of each year's cake partakers. This serves as moral boost for greater performance. God knows and does better. Though we were not partners with God during creation yet He gives us rights to the profit of the earth.

No one has the sole right or monopoly to the earth's resources. As a matter of fact no one can gain the whole world. That's why the Lord asked what it will profit you if you gain the whole world and lose your soul in hell (Matthew 16:26). The owner of all things is the Lord God. And He is not partial in the distribution of the profit or resources of the earth.

The profit of the earth is for all who know how to play the game of tapping into the abundance of earth's resources. The profit of the earth is not for Presidents or the Chief Executives of companies only or for few privileged ones. It is not equally for those who specialize in looting the treasury of the nations –theirs is ill gotten wealth and the end is nothing but certain destruction.

According to the word of the Lord, the profit of the earth is meant for everyone, the poorest of the poor inclusive.

> *"Moreover the profit of the earth is for all: the king himself is served by the field." (Ecclesiastes 5:9 KJV)*

Though the profit of the earth is for all but you must have the key to unlock and access the resources of the earth. Basically, God operates through principles and laws. Seek to know God's financial principles and apply them and that is the essence of this book. Remember that any area of your life that you shed the light of knowledge on will definitely be illuminated bringing forth outlandish improvements. You can't sail against the tide and expect to have a smooth sail. But if you follow through the direction of the tide you will not have tumultuous but safe journey.

The earth's resources to man is scarce but they are enough for plenteous living and enjoyment for all. Sad enough only few have known the laws of the game of prosperity and are controlling much of the earth's resources. And many others are just patching and struggling to survive. **You have your portion of the earth's riches. Don't live out your life cheated.** Be a partaker of the profits of the earth and not an onlooker.

5. Money is needed for kingdom expansion

The Gospel of our Lord and Saviour Jesus Christ is free but the channels for spreading it are expensive. According to divine injunction the gospel of our Lord and Saviour Jesus Christ must be preached to all the nations of the earth. Though the gospel is free yet it is preached at great cost both humanly and materially.

In our days the gospel is transmitted to millions of homes through satellite, internet, radio and television networks which require millions of naira to maintain. Money is needed to print Bibles, tracts and kingdom publications and to sponsor crusades. The missionaries who hazard their lives in various missionary fields across the globe must be catered for. Comfortable church buildings are needed in places of worship. As recorded in the Bible the Centurion for example built temple of worship with money not with mere military bravado or pomposity.

> *"And a certain centurion's servant, who was dear unto him, was sick, and ready to die.*
>
> *And when he heard of Jesus, he sent unto him the elders of the Jews, beseeching him that he would come and heal his servant. And when they came to Jesus, they besought him instantly, saying, that he was worthy for whom he should do this: For he loveth our nation, <u>and he hath built us a synagogue</u>." (Luke 7:1-5 KJV)*

Barnabas and many others meaningfully contributed to the welfare of the church members as recorded in Acts of the Apostles.

> *"And Joses, who was also named Barnabas by the apostles (which is translated Son of Encouragement), a Levite of the country of Cyprus, having land, sold it, and brought the money and laid it at the apostles' feet." (Acts 4:36-37 NKJV)*

Barnabas did not become son of encouragement with empty hands. His givings met needs in the Church, brought succour to many and created many demonstrations of gratefulness that ascended to the throne room in heaven.

When Israel sinned and God sent death in the land which claimed seventy thousand men in one day, David at the command of the Lord built an altar to offer sacrifice so that the plague would be stayed. Specific instruction was to build the altar at threshing floor of Araunah the Jebusite. David couldn't do otherwise. He paid for the parcel of land for building the altar to the Lord. He did not use his exalted and kingly position or government power to confiscate the land; he paid for it.

> *"And the king said unto Araunah, Nay; but I will surely buy it of thee at a price: neither will I offer burnt offerings unto the LORD my God of that which doth cost me nothing. So David bought the threshing floor and the oxen for fifty shekels of silver.*
>
> *And David built there an altar unto the LORD, and offered burnt offerings and peace offerings. So the LORD was intreated for the land, and the plague was stayed from Israel." (2 Sam 24:24-25 KJV)*

We need finances to buy public address systems and befitting musical instruments for praise and worship in our local Churches. You would not walk into any musical shop and order the owner to part with his items of trade. If you do you will be seen as a psychiatric patient. You need good money to have quality musical equipment. There are the needy, orphans and widows to care for in the land. The ministers of the gospel and other church workers must be adequately catered for to minister without distractions. All these needs and many more require finance.

> *"Neither was there any among them that lacked: for as many as were possessors of lands or houses sold them, and brought the prices of the things that were sold, And laid them down at the apostles' feet: and distribution was made unto every man according as he had need."(Acts 4:34-35 NJV)*

The resources will not come from outside the Church. They will come through the members of the body of Christ and that is why there must be financial pillars and not only spiritual pillars in every local congregation. And you are one of those financial pillars awaiting manifestation to play a key role in spreading the word of the kingdom.

6. God rejoices in the prosperity of His servants

Any one who thinks that poverty pleases God is making a very big mistake. In fact the person is dead wrong. No where in the infallible word of God was it written that God is pleased when you are afflicted and frustrated by poverty. When Israel was under Egyptian servitude their sorrows attracted God to intervene with strong arms. He judged Egyptian wickedness and delivered the people and led them to the land of economic freedom.

God is magnified when you increase. Conversely, it grieves God when you live beggarly as one without a Father.

> *"Let them shout for joy and be glad, who favor my righteous cause; and let them say continually, "Let the LORD be magnified, who has pleasure in the prosperity of His servant." (Psalm 35:27 NKJV)*

Oh praise God! God is pleased when you prosper. He is not the God of stagnancy and retrogression. He is the God of multiple increases who delights evermore in the progressive advancements of His servants and not in the misery of their financial wretchedness. In Psalm 35:26, God proclaimed confusion to all that rejoice over your hurts including poverty. And in the following verse He called for celebration among those who rejoice in His vindictive judgment against poverty and forces of darkness.

In fact God said His goodness will be a sign post showcasing His name upon us. Prosperity is part of God's goodness.

> *"And the LORD said, "I will cause all my goodness to pass in front of you, and I will proclaim my name, the LORD, in your presence. I will have mercy on whom I will have mercy, and I will have compassion on whom I will have compassion."*
>
> *(Exodus 33:19 NIV)*

At your front is God's goodness. At your back is the combination of His goodness and mercy. ***You are sandwiched with God's goodness so from where is the contamination of poverty?***

7. God gives power to make wealth

Making wealth is not necessarily by working the hardest but you must work. The Lord commands that you should not eat if you refuse to work (2 Thessalonians 3:10). Yes diligence and smart work are essential ingredients needed to increase in life. But it is God that gives power to make wealth. God will not throw down wealth to you from heaven but He gives you the power, the idea, the insight, the good health, the connection, etc, to generate the wealth. This God given ability is not just muscular display of strength. Because there are many that possess real physical strength and vigour and yet they are very poor. (Few have gainfully profited out of their physical strength). Thus you need to trust God for creative ideas. Every thing you see is an off shoot of an idea. It first existed in somebody's mind. So when you receive and build on any insight from the Lord, you are sure on the path of profit.

God gives the power to produce wealth in confirmation to His covenant which He swore to uphold by the immutability of His word and name.

> *"But remember the LORD your God, for it is he who gives you the ability to produce wealth, and so confirms his covenant, which he swore to your forefathers, as it is today." (Deuteronomy 8:18 NIV)*

Your wealth creative abilities confirm God's covenant. Ability to produce wealth is one of five power dimensions that God makes available to those that believe in him. (Other power dimensions are: power of Sonship (John 1:12), power to witness (Acts 1:8), power to trample on the enemies (Luke 10:19) and power of godliness (2 Peter 1:3)). This power is available but it will amount to nothing if you don't do any thing with it. *There is a God given idea in you which is latent. Activate it and the glory of your rising shall rend the heavens.*

8. God is a Great Investor and we should not be different

God is a great investor. Everything He does produces increase, be it spiritual, material and otherwise. With God there is nothing like diminishing returns. He invested in the salvation of the world by sacrificing His Son on the cross. And great is the bountiful harvest.

In Genesis 3:14, He declared His decision to invest in the deliverance of man from the shackles of Satan, sin, sickness, poverty and death. About four thousand years after this prophetic pronouncement, Jesus Christ was offered on the cross at Calvary. The ultimate return was total redemption of man. All that believe in Christ are living proofs to this.

God called out Abraham and made him father of many nations. It is only God that knows with certainty the great number of Abraham's seeds all over the world today. He said except a seed of corn is planted, it remains alone. But when it is planted, it brings increase.

> *"I tell you the truth, unless a kernel of wheat falls to the ground and dies, it remains only a single seed. But if it dies, it produces many seeds." John 12:24 (NIV)*

God in this Scripture speaks with the mind of an investor. Except you plant your seed it bears no fruit. ***Except you venture out, you risk losing what you already have.*** There is more danger in holding back your seed than in sowing same. God equally explained that one of the essential ingredients in investment is the expectation of returns and that is why He commands us to invest in hope (1 Corinthians 9:10).

In Psalm 126:5-6 the Lord talks about the pains of sowing and joy associated with reaping. This is true in business investments as well as in soul winning. We can't be different from our Father. Every seed produces after its kind. Lion gives birth to lion, Sheep to sheep and goat to goat. God is a great investor and we shouldn't be different if we are His.

> *"They that sow in tears shall reap in joy. He that goeth forth and weepeth, bearing precious seed, shall doubtless come again with rejoicing, bringing his sheaves with him. (Psalms 126:5-6 (KJV)*

Paul asserts that God gives increase to our plantations (1 Corinthians 3:7). It only takes one who knows about increase to give increase and that person is God.

9. Abundance and famine is part of life

It is a fact of life that there will always be seasons of famine and abundance. It is only those that plan against famine that survive the scourge. Temporary famine is not a problem but permanent famine (poverty) is a great scourge. Egypt had seven years of famine preceded by seven years of plenty. Was it not that they planned ahead with their abundance of seven years; words may not be enough to describe the harrowing consequences that would have resulted from the famine.

> *"It is just as I said to Pharaoh: God has shown Pharaoh what he is about to do. Seven years of great abundance are coming throughout the land of Egypt, but seven years of famine will follow them. Then all the abundance in Egypt will be forgotten, and the famine will ravage the land. The abundance in the land will not be remembered, because the famine that follows it will be so severe. (Genesis 41:28-31 NIV)*

Understand that time of financial adversity will definite come your way but how you survive in such times depends on what you make out of what you have now. But definitely the God that caused increase in Egypt during the seven years of plenty, the God that gave the dream and the interpretation to Pharoah released grace on Israel not to be consumed by poverty. ***Other nations probably had similar increase at the same time that Egypt blossomed but lacked the insight to prepare for rainy day.*** God will lead you to abundance that will serve as hedge in the days of famine.

10. Poverty is the destroyer of the poor

> *"The rich man's wealth is his strong city; the destruction of the poor is their poverty."*
>
> *(Proverbs 10:15 NKJV)*

You can't beat this Scripture. The poor man is destroyed by poverty. If you choose to remain poor, understand this that certain destruction is awaiting. How soon the destruction will occur is a matter of time. On the flip side, a rich man is protected strongly by his prosperity.

Thus while the poor are literally destroyed by poverty as exposed through the Scripture cited above, the rich are protected by their prosperity. ***What frightens the poor doesn't worry the rich.*** As a wise son of the kingdom you should rather choose to be rich than to remain in abject poverty and wait for this foretold and avoidable but certain destruction.

11. God teaches us to profit

"Thus says the LORD, your Redeemer, the Holy One of Israel: "I am the LORD your God, Who teaches you to profit, Who leads you by the way you should go."

(Isaiah 48:17 NKJV)

God is a great teacher who not only teaches on spiritual matters but instructs us on all issues of life. His eternal words contain life changing principles which are profitable in all spheres of life. When we diligently follow His leadings the resultant effects will be contentment, blessings and blissful end.

The Scripture quoted above is unambiguous in stating that God teaches us to profit. To profit means to make gain in your merchandise. The owner of all things, the Lord God of heaven and earth, had purchased us from the devil, sin and poverty, and if we follow His instructions we will definitely end up prosperous.

In God's School of Profit dishonesty, sharp practices, false balances, corruption and stealing are not allowed. Uprightness is one of the essential requirements in God's school of profit.

"Mark the blameless man, and observe the upright; for the future of that man is peace." (Psalms 37:37 NKJV)

Secure your future by walking uprightly. Shun vices that are ravaging and destroying many in the land today. What you have to do now is to enroll in God's School of Profit and you will be glad you did. Don't gain affluence by dubious means. You will lose all at the end. ***Prosperity is guaranteed if you trust and obey God.***

12. God abhors unfruitfulness

Jesus while on earth performed one miracle of judgment over an unfruitful fig tree.

Jesus' hope of getting fruits from this particular fig tree that had attributes of fruitfulness was dashed when he discovered the fig tree was all leaves and no fruits – symptomatic of all actions and no results. Consequently, he cursed the fig tree in demonstration of how God abhors barrenness -resistance to growth and increase.

The word of God says that none shall be unfruitful in the territory or domain of those who serve Him.

> *"There shall nothing cast their young, nor be barren, in thy land: the number of thy days I will fulfill." (Exodus 23:26 KJV)*

Poverty is retrogressive, oppressive and destructive. It gives no joy to any one. Dislike it as God disdains it. You cannot afford to accommodate barrenness when your Lord abhors it.

13. God lifted many in times past and is still lifting people today

God is a specialist in turning the poor, rejected and the forgotten of all ages to men of great renown -men of substance. He casts one down and lifts up another. With God the 'zeroes' are turned to 'heroes'. Nobody becomes amazing and extraordinary somebody. God has the sole right and power to cast one down and lift up the other. He did this in the time past; He is doing same today and will ever do it. Abraham, the father of faith was dependent on his father, Terah, even after marrying Sarah for both direction and sustenance (Genesis 11:26-32). Abraham was a complete failure and had bitter tales before he met God. But an encounter with God at the age of seventy five and continual fellowship ushered him to unprecedented spiritual and material blessings with peace of mind.

The Bible in Genesis 13:2 said: *"And Abram was very rich in cattle, in silver, and in gold."* And after Isaac was born the scriptures had this testimony of Abraham:

> *"And Abraham was old, and well stricken in age: and the LORD had blessed Abraham in all things." (Genesis 24:1 KJV)*

It was God that blessed Abraham in all things, that same God is alive and will visit to bless you in all your ways if only you trust in Him. ***It does not matter how long you have fallen, do not remain on the floor, rise up and trust God for lifting.***

Jacob who later in life became wealthier than his progenitors started out in his journey of prosperity with just a staff. After God had changed his situation he had this to say:

> *"I am not worthy of the least of all the mercies, and of all the truth, which thou hast shewed unto thy servant; for with my staff I passed over this Jordan; and now I am become two bands." (Genesis 32:10 KJV)*

David was the seventh son of Jesse, regarded as nobody by his brothers and was not even deemed fit to belong to the elitist army of Saul. He only found companion with the sheep in the thick bush. Yet he was lifted from the bush to the palace. It took God to locate and anoint him, before introducing him to Israel through killing of Goliath and subsequently made him King over all Israel. That same God will lift you up.

In our contemporary times God is prospering many who are attuned to His instructions (I am a living witness) and will continue to lift many others till the end of age. ***You are the next to be lifted.***

14. The righteous shall prosper always

The righteous shall be fruitful in season and out of season. Dryness shall be far away from those that trust in God. Delight and walk in the laws of the Lord and you shall have good success.

> *"Blessed is the man, Who walks not in the counsel of the ungodly, nor stands in the path of sinners, nor sits in the seat of the scornful; but his delight is in the law of the LORD, And in His law he meditates day and night. He shall be like a tree planted by the rivers of water, that brings forth its fruit in its season, whose leaf also shall not wither; and whatever he does shall prosper." (Psalm 1:1-3 NKJV)*

Delighting yourself in the law of the Lord and refusing to make money through ungodly means will enable you to contact the grace to prosper in all your works. In God you are a fruitful bough and will never be unproductive. The righteous is likened to a palm tree whose every part is useful. Your every part shall be fruitful alike in the mighty name of Jesus and at old age you will not be a liability but you will still remain fruitful.

> *"The righteous shall flourish like a palm tree; He shall grow like a cedar in Lebanon.*
>
> *Those who are planted in the house of the LORD shall flourish in the courts of our God. They shall still bear fruit in old age; they shall be fresh and flourishing, to declare that the LORD is upright; He is my rock, and there is no unrighteousness in Him." (Psalm 92:12-15 NKJV)*

Because you are involved actively and righteously in kingdom affairs, **you have won all court cases against poverty.** God is not unrighteous to reward all your labours with failure. As cedars of Lebanon towers higher than every other tree you shall be valuable and recognizable.

15. Money Answers ALL

We see, feel, and touch money in every day living. Acting as though money does not matter is hypocritical and illusionary. Given, money cannot buy the air we breathe, salvation and heaven. But these are among the few extremes that money cannot buy. As a matter of fact you need money virtually for all other things necessary for our comfort while we live. Money is needed to put food on the table. You need money to organize party and buy wine for merriment.

The power of money is so strong that the Scripture declares that money answers all things. In other words there is so much you can do with money.

> *"A feast is made for laughter, and wine maketh merry: but money answereth all things." (Ecclesiastes 10: 19 KJV)*

You may not even understand that you can use money to buy laughter. If in doubt then ask those that organize nights of thousand laughs and you will be shocked to know that huge sums of money are really paid handsomely for these shows.

16. Wealth Has Many Friends, Poverty is A Destitute

"Wealth maketh many friends; but the poor is separated from his neighbour."

(Proverbs 19: 4 KJV)

"The poor is hated even of his own neighbour: but the rich hath many friends."

(Proverbs 14: 20 KJV)

The rich have retinue of friends, followers and admirers and this is because people like to associate with success. Conversely the poor is despised even by his neighbours because of poverty irrespective of his wisdom. The presence of the poor places a demand on his resources. Probably the neighbour of the poor may not intentionally despise him but because **poverty is repulsive and carries along with it the aura of disconnection.** It is this aura of disconnection that brings despising. After all the affluent neighbour may say is the poor not part of the problem instead of being part of the solution?

17. Money is A Strong Defense

"The rich man's wealth is his strong city ..." *(Proverbs 18: 11 KJV)*

From the Scripture quoted above to build the wall of defense you have to build the wall of prosperity. Money indeed is good and answers to many problems. Don't make mistake about this you need money but your trust should be in the Lord. Because of the fame that prosperity attracts, many unscrupulously get rich. Some kill and others loot the treasury of their organizations or Countries. But the wealth gotten through foul means serves as a curse and destroyer to its victims. **Wealth gotten out of labour is sweet and lasts.**

18. God gives bread to the eater and seed to the sower

"For as the rain cometh down, and the snow from heaven, and

returneth not thither, but watereth the earth, and maketh it bring forth and bud, that it may give seed to the sower, and bread to the eater: So shall my word be that goeth forth out of my mouth: it shall not return unto me void, but it shall accomplish that which I please, and it shall prosper in the thing whereto I sent it." (Isaiah 55:10-11KJV)

Bread is to the eater, while seed is to the sower! The central question is who are you?

Are you a sower or an eater? ***Many have devoured the seeds that could have made them great in life.*** And at the time of harvest they have no fields to harvest.

What you have in your hands could be turned to either bread or seed depending on your mind set or who you are. The money that passes through your hand each passing day could be eaten as bread; it could equally be invested to create additional seeds. The bread eaten today turns to waste tomorrow but the seed sown today engenders hope of a great harvest tomorrow.

God does not expect you to be a bread eater only that is why He created the earth for you to plant and be sure He will cause increase in your vineyards.

19. Prosperity and Pleasures all the way

Are you a servant of the Lord? Are you equally obedient to Him? Then hear this!

"If they obey and serve him, they shall spend their days in prosperity, and their years in pleasures." (Job 36:11 KJV)

The Lord said that any of His servants that are obedient will live in prosperity each passing day. In other words every day that berths is destined for the increase of those that serve the Lord. Since I discovered this portion of the word I wake up everyday conscious of walking in prosperity. The prosperity of the days accumulates to the year long pleasures. These are prosperities without attachments or undertones.

"The blessing of the Lord, it maketh rich, and he addeth no sorrow with it." (Proverbs 10:22 KJV)

There is nothing like a bad day or year for those that honour the Lord. Notice that the daily prosperity and yearly pleasures are not confined to some particular seasons, age bracket, race or sex. Even at old age you shall not be tired of life due to hardship, sickness and poverty. You shall be surrounded with pleasures.

20. Seasons of sowing and reaping

The Lord created times and seasons. Each season heralds a distinct purpose and those that recognize the essence of each season and makes the maximum use of such stands to increase. There is the season of sowing. There is equally the season of reaping and reward. God through nature is calling on you to rise up to sowing. It is the responsibility of man to sow while God gives the increase.

"While the earth remaineth, seed time and harvest, and cold and heat, and summer and winter, and day and night shall not cease." (Genesis 8: 22 KJV)

This is a law that must be obeyed by any one who wishes to wriggle out of poverty or wishes to keep increasing. Whosoever that sows gets to reap. Any one who fails to sow will have nothing to reap. Put succinctly, any one that fails to cast his seeds will not cast the sickle at harvest times. It is imperative to point that any one that breaks this law does so at his own peril. **The rich are consistently sowing and increasing so why should any one who wishes to be free from the shackles of poverty refuse to sow?**

21.. Overrunning Cup

"Thou preparest a table before me in the presence of mine enemies: thou anointest my head with oil; my cup runneth over." (Psalm 23:5 KJV)

You cannot have an overrunning cup and not prosper. Over flowing cup is symptomatic of prosperity. There is a release in the heavens triggering off a spill over effect in your wealth creation. **Get ready, your biggest container now is too small for the over flow that is coming.**

Chapter 2

JESUS' PARABLE OF MONEY

Jesus Christ taught much about money making and management in the parable of talents in Matthew Chapter Twenty Five. More often than none this parable is given interpretations from various pulpits that is limited to spiritual endowments given for the benefit of the Church which does not make less potent the financial lessons contained therein.

We grew up hearing our Pastors preaching from this portion of the Scriptures and never were mention made of financial principles clearly spelt out by the Master of the Talents Himself. But we know much better now. The talent was the measure of monetary currency in the days of Jesus. So this parable also is about money.

From the parable we will have God's standpoints on creative enterprising and the pains associated with financial ignorance and failings. *Those who dare to venture win, while those who laze about only add to the increase of those already have.* There are at least twenty lessons on finance derivable from this parable of talents by Jesus.

> *"For the kingdom of heaven is like a man traveling to a far country, who called his own servants and delivered his goods to them. And to one he gave five talents, to another two, and to another one, to each according to his own ability; and immediately he went on a journey. Then he who had received the five talents went and traded with them, and made another five talents. And likewise he who had received two gained two more also. But he who had received*

one went and dug in the ground, and hid his lord's money. After a long time the lord of those servants came and settled accounts with them. So he who had received five talents came and brought five other talents, saying, 'Lord, you delivered to me five talents; look, I have gained five more talents besides them.' "His lord said to him, 'Well done, good and faithful servant; you were faithful over a few things, I will make you ruler over many things. Enter into the joy of your lord.' "He also who had received two talents came and said, 'Lord, you delivered to me two talents; look, I have gained two more talents besides them.' "His lord said to him, 'Well done, good and faithful servant; you have been faithful over a few things, I will make you ruler over many things. Enter into the joy of your lord.' "Then he who had received the one talent came and said, 'Lord, I knew you to be a hard man, reaping where you have not sown, and gathering where you have not scattered seed. And I was afraid, and went and hid your talent in the ground. Look, there you have what is yours.' "But his lord answered and said to him, 'You wicked and lazy servant, you knew that I reap where I have not sown, and gather where I have not scattered seed. So you ought to have deposited my money with the bankers, and at my coming I would have received back my own with interest. Therefore take the talent from him, and give it to him who has ten talents. For to everyone who has, more will be given, and he will have abundance; but from him who does not have, even what he has will be taken away. And cast the unprofitable servant into the outer darkness. There will be weeping and gnashing of teeth." (Matthew 25:14–30 NKJV)

1. You Are God's Servant in Financial Matters As Well As In Other Areas of Services to Him.

"For the kingdom of heaven is like a man traveling to a far country, <u>who called his own servants</u>" (Verse 14). The Scripture is very clear here. You are God's servant. Any one entrusted with the responsibility of managing resources is a steward to the one who hired him. God is the owner and giver of all resources. We are only stewards entrusted with the management of these resources. As a servant you don't have all of God's resources. You can only get a part to manage.

Also as God's servant, it is expected of you to be faithful in the discharge of this responsibility. The Scripture states that, *"it is required in stewards that one be found faithful." (1 Corithians4:2 NKJV)*

No management will commit greater resources to any manager who is irresponsible and unaccountable. But because managers know that they are accountable to those who appointed them, discretion, prudence, diligence and faithfulness are employed in managing both human and material resources for their various organizations.

When you understand that you are accountable to God even in money matters, you will be very prudent in carrying out this function. I dare to say that if you are unfaithful in money matters your faithfulness in other areas of service may be suspect. Thus discharge your duties in all areas of calling as unto the Lord.

2. The Money You Have Belongs To God and Must Be Used In Ways That Honour Him

The finances that come to you are never your own, **you are just money manager who is accountable to God on the utilization of the resources.** The Scripture says that the *"man...... delivered his goods to them."* (Matthew 25:14)

When you know that the money you have is part of God's blessings you will employ the money in meaningful projects that will yield increases to the praise of God. The money will be used in ways that glorify God. You will not use it to oppress the poor or to work against the purpose of God. Also money will be your servant and not the other way round. **Very importantly, the understanding that all your possessions belong to God will equally help you so that the gold will not turn to be your god.** God has delivered his goods to you! What are you making out of them?

3. God Gives Based On Our Different and Several Abilities

"And to one he gave five talents, to another two, and to another one, to each according to his own ability; and immediately he went on a journey." (Matthew 25:15)

God will not give you what will destroy you. He gives based on the size of your container. **When you deepen your ability to manage the resources committed to you, more resources will be committed into your hands.** We have received different start up capital from the Lord. And the truth is that the little you have received is enough to put you on the part of abundance if only you dare to start now and be prudent and diligent in deploying such resources.

4. You Have the Latitude to Manage What Has Been Committed Into Your Hands

"And to one he gave five talents, to another two, and to another one, to each according to his own ability; and immediately he went on a journey."(Matthew 25:15)

The Lord will not stand over you to dictate to what uses you are to put the resources. He gives you the free hand to run. But the wise will always seek His guidance before launching out. Recall, after the father of the prodigal son (Luke 15:11-32) gave him the share of his inheritance he left the son to the management of same. Unfortunately, the son was extravagant and squandered what was given to him and thus resorted to eating husks meant for swine. **If you don't wish to eat from the dung hill of poverty ensure to manage prudently the resources you have on hand right now.**

5. Money Can Be Grown and You Need Combination of Enterprising Skills to Grow It

"Then he who had received the five talents went and traded with them, and made another five talents. And likewise he who had received two gained two more also." (Matthew 25:16-17)

The servants that received five and two talents respectively immediately ventured into trade. This entails they were involved in commercial and economic activities of buying and selling and they grew because they sold more and spent less. So **you must spend less than you earn if you must grow your finances.** Master the principles of any trade, acquire the skills and practice same over time and you will become successful. **And the secret which is really no secret is to involve only in businesses with incremental and measurable returns.**

6. The Poor and Rich Think Differently On Monetary Matters

"And likewise he who had received two gained two more also. But he who had received one went and dug in the ground, and hid his lord's money." (Matthew 25:17-18)

Whilst the men that received five and two units of money straightly went into trading, the man that received less put his money to an unfruitful use. He dug ground and buried the money. The truth is that both those that received more and less put their receipts to use but the difference was while the rich sought ways to increase, the poor put the money into wrong uses that reduced the worth. **The same is true today, whenever the man with rich mentality receives any money, he thinks of better ways to grow the money. But when the poor receives any money what comes to mind first is how to spend the money.**

7. Money Should Be Grown Over Time

"After a long time the lord of those servants came..................." *(Matthew 25:19)*

Money grows. This should be over time. Run away from hot money or be hurt by it. Invest ₦5,000 today and gain ₦100 million tomorrow is never cheap. Aim at progressive enrichment. Build wealth over time, avoid get rich quick syndrome that is pervading the land today. This has destroyed values of integrity, hard work and honest gains. You cannot go this way and be clean and unhurt.

"A faithful man will abound with blessings, but he who hastens to be rich will not go unpunished. A man with an evil eye hastens after riches, and does not consider that poverty will come upon him." (Proverbs 28:20-22 NKJV)

Many who are hasty in gaining money and fame through unscrupulous means never live long to enjoy the loot. The Lord of the servants came back after a long time and the servants were still in business. The servants were in a business with potentials and a future.

8. Keep Records of Your Financial Transactions

".......the lord of those servants came and settled accounts with them." (Matthew 25:19)

When the master of those servants returned from his trip they all gathered to render accounts of their performance. One interesting thing about this is that both those that gained and the man who did not increase gave account on how they handled the money given to them.

Endeavour to monitor your incomes and expenses. And one sure way of doing this is to have records of your financial dealings. Buy exercise books to track your finances. The easier option which is more appealing is not to write at all. *The danger of keeping no records is that you will not be able to determine while there is still time with certainty if you are progressing or retrogressing.* Be interested and detailed in knowing what happens to the money in your hands.

9. The Rich Have Abundance Mentality

"..........'Lord, you delivered to me five talents; look, I have gained five more talents besides them.' (Matthew 25:20 & 22)

The servants with five and two talents where satisfied with the quantity and quality of gifts they received from their Master and that was why they were not ashamed in reporting back to their Master that "you gave us five and two talents respectively, behold we have gained additional five and two." (Paraphrase mine). From the testimonies they re-affirmed that their Master owns both them and the material resources.

No matter what you have it's only but a little of God's unlimited resources. *The man with abundance thinking believes that there is enough space at the top for every one that aspires to move up.* I am not sure you have seen any two birds colliding in mid air. It is only on the ground that you see squabbles and ungodly practices aimed at undermining one another. There is enough room at the top for everyone. What the man with five talents gained could not serve as a preclusion to what others gained. Except the man with one talent, others toiled graciously without witch hunting one another or name calling and God blessed their labours. Your right labour shall be sweet.

10. Riches Create a Sense of Happiness and Boldness

"His lord said to him, 'Well done, good and faithful servant; you were faithful over a few things, I will make you ruler over many things. Enter into the joy of your lord." (Matthew 25:21&23)

Appraisal is an integral part of life. It is a time of evaluation and rewards.

Those that do well in organizations receive pat on the back by ways of commendations and promotions while those that are laggards usually receive some beating by way of queries, warnings, demotions and sack. Performance measurement and management was copied from the Bible by Management Consultants.

The two servants that increased their wealth were ushered into the happiness and joy of prosperity. There is this common saying that wealth gives measure of confidence. If you have fifty thousand naira (₦50, 000) in your bank account and there comes an adversity of ₦50, 000, what you will simply do is to boldly go to your bank account, withdraw the money and solve the problem. You will not be submerged in fear as to where and how to get the money to solve the problem. You will not go a begging neither will you come back sorrowing. The servants boldly walked up to their Master to render account of stewardship. They were not arrogant while giving account of their dealings. Thus in your boldness you must display humility. The servants were humble because God gives grace to the humble but resists the proud. ***The truly rich are bold and not really arrogant*** knowing fully well that all they have is but a gift from the Lord.

11. Faithfulness in Handling the Little Money You Have Now or Otherwise Determines Increase or Decrease

"His lord said to him, <u>you were faithful over a few things, I will make you ruler over many things</u>.' (Matthew 25: 21)

More talents were handed over to the men that gained five and two incremental talents to manage. *The blessings of God may start with additions but as we prove faithful they will increase in multiples.* For those that proved faithful in managing their little start up capital additional funds were handed over to them. The Bible says: *"You were faithful over a few things, I will make you ruler over many things."* As they traded in small measures of money, they got experiences through mistakes made and through skills acquired while practicing their trades they developed their capacities to handle more resources before much was committed into their hands. Conversely, the man that was unfaithful was stripped of the little he had and he became yet poorer.

12. To the Poor Every Progressing Man Is A Cheat, Thief or Corrupt.

"Then he who had received the one talent came and said, 'Lord, I knew you to be a hard man, reaping where you have not sown, and gathering where you have not scattered seed. Matthew 25:24

Most times many people are quick in condemning those doing well financially. This may not be far from the fact that we live in a perverse age where corrupt enrichment is rampant. Get this right, not every one doing well financially increased through ritualistic, dubious or corrupt means. Many of them increased through honest means because they knew the rules of money and applied same in their endeavours. *They are only castigated by the ignorant just like the Master in this parable who was vilified by the ignorant poor servant over his mastery in financial affairs. If you despise the genuinely rich in your heart, you are invariably scorning riches. And this is dangerous as you can't attract what you hate.*

13. It Is Those Not Doing Well Financially That Complain Usually About Money.

"And I was afraid, and went and hid your talent in the ground. Look, there you have what is yours."(Matthew 25: 25)

The man who put his money to wrong use was the only one among the servants that was filled with fear, bitterness, murmuring and complains. He accused his Master of being a slave driver, a thief and a cheat. But he was mistaken. What he did not know was that probably as his master invested in him, the Master may have invested on other ventures –possibly the Master bought shares in companies also. Being a shareholder does not entitle the Master to be involved in the day to day operations of the company. So the servant never saw the Master going to those companies in the course of the year to direct on how to handle the affairs of the organizations. This is absolutely unnecessary. There is a management team on ground to do this. But the Master was entitled to receive dividend based on his investments every year. So as this poor servant watched his Master receive returns upon returns from business ventures he had invested in, he ignorantly concluded that the Master was really a hard man, reaping where he never sowed. ***Remove the judgmental cloak from your eyes; don't be bitter at other peoples success, then you will see clearly to move forward.***

14. The Poor Are Afraid To Invest or Embark On New Ventures

"<u>And I was afraid</u>, and went and hid your talent in the ground."
Matthew 25:25

Most poor are risk averse and obsessed with fear of failure. But one of the underlying principles of investment is no risk no returns; the higher the risk the higher the returns and the lower the risk, the lower the returns. Everything in life involves taking risk so why shun doing something new? Your lying down to sleep is risky because there is no guarantee that you are going to wake up the next morning anyway, yet you still take the risk to sleep. Your leaving house in the morning to work is equally risky as there is no assurance that you will come home alive yet you go out anyway. So why not come off the veil of fear that has kept you tied down from advancing forward and do something new today. ***Risk taking is tantamount to working in faith when you cast your trust in God to prosper you in that new initiative you are about to launch into.*** Fear of the future and inability to learn skillful trade held this servant captive that he never ventured into new things. Fear is a destroyer and has inhibited many from realizing their full potentials. God has not given us the spirit of fear but of love and sound mind so confront the fear and move on to attain greatness not condemnation.

15. The Poor Possesses a Particular Frame Of Mind And Finds It Difficult To Embrace Changes

The man that buried his talent obviously saw his other two colleagues taking the trading options, but he never bothered to inquire or learn of what they were doing. His concern was that the master was hard. He was equally afraid of the unknown which stopped him from venturing out and eventually destroyed him. *Friends, its better to be a weak man and die in the battle field than to be a brave man who refuses to venture into battle field only to be slaughtered by the enemies in the home front of idleness.* Ask questions if you don't understand how others are increasing. Don't sit back to resent those progressing. This is why the Bible says in the multitude of counsels there is safety.

"For by wise counsel thou shalt make thy war: and in multitude of counselors there is safety."(Proverbs 24:6 KJV)

The world is littered with information and it is the informed that are transformed who incidentally become outstanding. It is only those that stand out that are recognized and celebrated.

16. The Lord Called This Poor Man Wicked and Lazy

"But his lord answered and said to him, 'You wicked and lazy servant, you knew that I reap where I have not sown, and gather where I have not scattered seed."

(Matthew 25:26)

The poor servant never attracted the sympathy of the Lord but outright condemnation. Why did the Lord call this servant with one talent wicked and lazy? He was wicked because he was wasteful and unappreciative of what God gave to him. He was lazy because he was hard working but never used his brain power. Let me explain the concept of laziness here which is different from our conventional definition of laziness which simply means "not hard working." I want to say that this poor man worked hardest among the servants. He was the only one that dug the ground to bury the talent. Either he tied the money in nylon to prevent spoilage by water or rodents or he plastered the hole before burying the money. Whichever way it took strength to dig the ground both to bury and bring out the money when the master requested for it. *He was full of uncreative and unfruitful hard labour. He misdirected his energy in ventures that never produced commendable results.* He was ungrateful and intelligibly bankrupt that was why he was called wicked and lazy.

17. The Poor Are Unable To Recognize Alternative Sources of Income

"......Then he who had received the five talents went and traded with them, ... So you ought to have deposited my money with the bankers, and at my coming I would have received back my own with interest...." (Matthew 25:16,27)

From the parable of talents there were two alternatives that the poor could have invested the money given unto him. He could have either traded with the money or fixed it in an interest yielding account with the bank. But he never did any of these. *There is plethora of opportunities in the investment spectrum which the rich choose from but the poor are stereotyped and fixated in one line of income.* The poor more often than not depend solely on fixed income jobs. The earlier you start to seek after multiple streams of income the better for you. You can have the job but seek to own the business.

18. The Poor Don't Know the Power of Savings and Compound Interest (Incremental Growth)

The Master said, "So you ought to have deposited my money with the bankers, and at my coming I would have received back my own with interest." Matthew 25:27. (NIV).

Every one with rich mentality knows the importance of savings and compound interest. The money put into unproductive use by being buried in the ground was prone to be eaten by rodents –inflation. But if he had fixed the money in interest yielding account, the interest earned would at least take care of the inflation while leaving the principal intact.

19. The Poor Will Always Contribute To the Increase of the Rich

"For to everyone who has, more will be given, and he will have abundance; but from him who does not have, even what he has will be taken away." (Matthew 25:29)

Since the rich will not break into the house of the poor to steal, just how then do the poor increase the rich? The Lord gave me insight into this portion of the Scriptures on how the poor contribute to the increase of the rich. Take for example most average men in the country today who are not really rich have at least two different phone lines either due to poor interconnectivity among the network operators or because of band wagon effect. These phones of necessity must be recharged with air time and at each point of recharge two things happen —money leaves one man's pocket and enters another man's pocket. Don't get me wrong, phone is important but for every phone recharge card purchased just to talk the rich smiles to the bank. Think about this! This may equally be happening in other areas of your life.

20. The Poor Are Always In the Regrettable and Dark Corner of Pains and Bitterness

"And cast the unprofitable servant into the outer darkness. There will be weeping and gnashing of teeth.' (Matthew 25:30 NKJV)

Two of the three servants who increased their wealth portfolio were joyful while the poor was banished into outer darkness of poverty, frustration and regrets. From the parable, poverty was associated with unfruitfulness, darkness, weeping and gnashing of teeth, while the prosperous servants were joyful and fulfilled. These are two sides of the coin. Thus **whosoever that says prosperity is not good should try poverty.**

The Lord in this timeless teaching is urging us to be resourceful, tactful and diligent in handling money matters. You can increase out of the little in your hands at the moment through knowledge and creative enterprising. As you do this you will avoid the pitfalls of poverty.

Chapter 3

ABRAHAM'S AND LAZARUS' PEOPLE

Broadly speaking there are two classes of people in the Church today when it comes to believing God for prosperity in their lives-the Abraham and the Lazarus people. The one group is positively orientated towards prosperity while the other group is negatively inclined towards prosperity and money matters. The one group professes their faith and believes God for material increment in whatever they lay hands on. And God is working wonders through them. This group incidentally is few. They are not biased in their belief of God. Their prosperity belief is all round, that is, they believe to prosper spiritually, materially and health wise.

The other set are those who though know God as their Lord and owner of all resources but find it difficult to believe that God's unlimited resources could be enjoyed liberally by them. These people tend to confess their unalloyed, undying belief in God but lack the working faith to attract and appropriate God's abundance. *Ignorance to a large extent is contributory to the imbalance in the areas of materiality and spirituality* among this group. Prosperity to them could be for every other person excluding them. They copied some aspects of Abraham's workings with God and failed to imbibe the whole tenets of that relationship.

The lyrics below are from one of the popular Christian songs in Nigeria:

"Abraham's blessings are mine,
I am blessed in the morning,
I am blessed in the evening Abraham's blessings are mine."

Every time there is an allusion to prosperity, the Christian suddenly remembers that he is an offspring of Abraham and by implications the blessings of Abraham automatically should belong to him. **Demonstrably no one by proclamations loves poverty, yet the actions or inactions of many bring poverty to them.** If riches only come by repeated confessions, then every Christian would have been materially rich. What we have is a paradox of many who claim to be rich for being Abraham's seed actually living dejectedly poor. But why claim to be Abraham's and live like Lazarus?

No Christian living or dead ever sung:

"Lazarus poverty is mine,
I am poor in the morning,
I am poor in the evening,
Lazarus poverty is mine"

While every Christian appreciates the piety of Lazarus none of them would ever wish to be associated with the state of dogs licking his wounds as a result of no means of sustenance and down trodden life.

There were two phases of Abraham's life -the pre and post seventy five year eras.

Abraham before God called him out at the age of seventy five was everything but success. Abraham was the first among the sons of Terah. In all ramifications Abraham before the setting in of the God factor was a total failure. This life changing encounter with God altered everything for his good. Thus **if God is with you, you have lost the right to fail.** The family of Abraham was traumatized and plagued with sorrow, pain, premature death and unfruitfulness.

From Genesis 11:26-31, we read that:

"Terah lived seventy years, and became the father of Abram, Nahor

and Haran. Now these are the records of the generations of Terah. Terah became the father of Abram, Nahor and Haran; and Haran became the father of Lot. Haran died in the presence of his father Terah in the land of his birth, in Ur of the Chaldeans. Abram and Nahor took wives for themselves. The name of Abram's wife was Sarai; and the name of Nahor's wife was Milcah, the daughter of Haran, the father of Milcah and Iscah. Sarai was barren; she had no child. Terah took Abram his son, and Lot the son of Haran, his grandson, and Sarai his daughter-in-law, his son Abram's wife; and they went out together from Ur of the Chaldeans in order to enter the land of Canaan; and they went as far as Haran, and settled there. (NASU)

Some facts are easily seen from the Scriptures above. First, Abram was the first among the three sons of Terah. Though being the first born could lead to inheriting much of his father's possessions traditionally speaking yet this position never conferred on him the right to succeed. *Your placement in the family tree may not necessary be a determining success factor.*

Second, their family had record and trace of premature death. Haran, the immediate younger brother to Abraham died before their father leaving behind Lot his son to the care of the father.

Third, Haran had a head start in life before Abraham. In their days the greatness of a man was largely a function of the size of the family and farm possessions. Haran before cold hands of death snatched him has had an issue well ahead of Abraham.

Fourth, all that Abraham embarked upon were not successful. Sarah, his wife was barren, unfruitful. This problem was only solved when the God factor set in. Abraham proved faithful in his twenty five years work with God before Isaac was born. So don't curse or deny God while waiting for His visitations.

Fifth, Abraham even after marriage was still dependent on his father for sustenance and direction. The Bible said in verse 27 of Genesis 11, that "Terah took Abram......" All the Scriptural translations consulted used the same words that, "Terah took Abram ......," connoting that at this point in time Abraham was not self reliant. Abraham and the wife were economically dependent on Terah, the father.

Sixth, the family had a history of truncated projects. Their father set out with his sons to the land of Canaan but ended in the land of Haran -very typical of unfinished business syndrome.

But these ugly conundrums changed when God stepped into Abraham's life. In Genesis chapter 12:1, Abraham began his work with God. As a result of this pleasant twist, "a poor man" became a rich man; a pagan zero was turned to a hero of faith; an unknown, insignificant man became very great and a blessing to the entire humanity; a friend of God and father of nations. In fact he became the father of faith. The God factor crushed the imprint of poverty and premature death in his family linage. Abraham rather than burying any of his sons was actually buried by the sons at good old age. Isaac, his son was buried by his sons also at good old age and Jacob the grandson of Abraham was equally buried in good old age by his sons. The debilitating effects of poverty that trailed and petrified Abraham's family before the setting in of the God factor were eliminated. The family became so blessed that nations became intimidated as a consequence of their affluence. God will visit you with mind blowing, net breaking blessings that will make the world to honour your God.

The Bible gave an indefatigable testimony that Abraham was blessed by God in all things.

> *"And Abraham was old, and well stricken in age: and the LORD had blessed Abraham in all things." (Gen 24:1 KJV).*

Abraham was an epitome of total success; an example of how God progressively blesses His people. He feared God and laid the foundation of faith for those who will truly serve God. Abraham was very great materially; Isaac was greater but Jacob was greatest. Jacob confirmed being greater that his progenitors when he was pronouncing latter days blessings on his descendants. (Genesis 49:26)

Building on the foundation of God's covenants Abraham was not lazy spiritually, mentally and vocationally. Manna never fell from heaven for him just as the days of Israel's pilgrimage in the desert yet he was stupendously rich. Abraham was involved in the merchandise of goods which were in common demand everyday in his days. He was involved in haulage business transporting agricultural produce from the farm to places of need. *Abraham invested in precious stones that appreciate over time and not subject to inflation and loss of value.* Their days were such that the enemies could attack any moment. And what did Abraham do? He had servants who were both employees and trained soldiers. He had great measure of military fortification and monetary defense and creditably served, obeyed and never robbed God by withholding his tithe.

What about Lazarus?

"There was a rich man who was dressed in purple and fine linen and lived in luxury every day. At his gate was laid a beggar named Lazarus, covered with sores and longing to eat what fell from the rich man's table. Even the dogs came and licked his sores. "The time came when the beggar died and the angels carried him to Abraham's side. The rich man also died and was buried. In hell, where he was in torment, he looked up and saw Abraham far away, with Lazarus by his side. So he called to him, 'Father Abraham, have pity on me and send Lazarus to dip the tip of his finger in water and cool my tongue, because I am in agony in this fire.'

"But Abraham replied, 'Son, remember that in your lifetime you received your good things, while Lazarus received bad things, but now he is comforted here and you are in agony. And besides all this, between us and you a great chasm has been fixed, so that those who want to go from here to you cannot, nor can anyone cross over from there to us." (Luke 16:19-26 NIV)

Lazarus in his life time greatly feared God as Abraham did but he was very, very poor materially. The Lord summed up Lazarus' earthly journey thus: "*...Lazarus received bad things....*" Lazarus was clothed with poverty that exposed him to ridicule. He could not provide for daily living, thus he resorted to begging for livelihood. He had

37

putrefying sores that needed medical attention but because there was no money for this, dogs licked the wounds wherever he went to beg. Lazarus died in abject poverty, humiliation and suffering. But because he feared God and not because he was poor, Lazarus went to heaven when he died. He never had part of God's best materially here on earth.

Because of the comparison in this story between the rich man who incidentally was a son of Abraham but failed to fear God and Lazarus who though feared God but lived in ridiculous poverty, many erroneously think that this story teaches to be poor in order to make heaven. It is useless living and falsely consoling self that is better going through life poor in order to make heaven than being rich and end up missing heaven. Don't live with the illusion that heaven is mainly for the materially poor because your definition of "poor" is different from God's classified or advocated "poor in the spirit." Understand that Abraham enjoyed heaven on earth and is resting in paradise, while Lazarus was traumatized and stigmatized by poverty here on earth though he equally ended up in heaven because he feared God and kept His word in his little strength and not because he was poor. The most probable reason the rich man was kicked out of heaven was not because he was not the son of Abraham but because of his refusal to use the wealth committed into his hands to serve God and humanity. He trusted in the riches rather than God.

Don't live to beg bread because it casts doubt on the potency of God to provide for His own. *The availability of God cannot be exhausted not in time and even in eternity.* Refuse also to live beggarly because of erroneous belief that poverty is synonymous to fearing God. Don't equally end up poor with the illusion that the poor end up in heaven.

So you decide which group you belong to -Abraham's group or Lazarus' group. The choice is yours to make.

Discard Average Mentality

Agur in Proverbs 30:7-9 cried to God against poverty and excessive riches.

Two things I request of You (Deprive me not before I die): Remove falsehood and lies far from me; Give me neither poverty nor riches-- Feed me with the food allotted to me;

Lest I be full and deny You, And say, "Who is the LORD?" Or lest I be poor and steal, and profane the name of my God. (NKJV)

Agur probably in his days saw the debilitating effects of poverty and destructions from arrogance of riches. It appears also that he believed that the poor profane God and the rich deny Him. Thus he cried out that instead of being poor and or rich and consequently rebel against God, it would be better to be at the middle of the road: neither be poor nor be rich.

The prayer as good as it sounds is a prayer of one with average mentality who never expected to rise above a certain level in life. Aim above the sky that's where you belong. Who says that God is not able to uphold you in the midst of His stupendous abundance and provisions? Job in his days was the richest man in the East yet he feared God and eschewed evil. Isaac was so rich that he became the envy of the entire nation of Philistine. King Abimelech and his people had to enter into truce with Isaac because they saw the hand of God in his success. God is well able to preserve you in the midst of his provisions only trust and obey Him. Is He not the one that said that "upon every glory there is a defense? (Isaiah 4:5) Is He not equally the one who said the "blessings of the Lord maketh rich and added no sorrow to it? (Proverbs 10:22)

Debunking Fallacies about Riches

Let us take some space below to debunk some of the lies about riches.

1. Poverty Is Not Piety

Many have been deceived for so long to associate holiness with poverty. You cannot be rich and serve God they have been made to believe. What a poisonous and strangulating teaching you have swallowed. Nothing could be far from the truth. I have found out that most of the terrible wickedness in the land is carried out by the poor. These are master minds of pull him down (PhD) syndrome.

Because we are down, they say, so every other person must be down. When the young wants to rise to better living these men plot to destroy because they would have others to be poorer than they are despite their wretched state many of them even go diabolical to achieve their evil schemes. I declare that every hand holding you down be broken in Jesus name.

You can be rich and serve God faithfully. Examples abound from the infallible Word of God. Abraham was so strong and lavishly rich that his servants-turned-soldiers fought and overcame five kings and their armies. If Abraham was blessed, what would you say of Jacob? Jacob told of how he was blessed above his progenitors in the book of Genesis Chapter forty nine.

David was a shepherd boy that served God with unalloyed zeal in holiness and was made a king of Israel. God was his number one priority all the days of his life and for this he became a man after God's heart. Solomon was blessed with wisdom that unlocked the chambers of riches. The prosperity was transformational and not enslaving and in his days silver was like stones in the streets of Jerusalem (1 Kings 10:27)

Daniel was a great administrator in the Babylonian empire. His administrative ingenuity made him indispensable such that he operated under the reign of three different kings in two different empires. Succinctly put Daniel's influence and relevance transcended three kingdoms. Yet in all these he was faithful to God.

Paul was a lawyer by profession, a tent maker by occupation and a preacher by calling yet he served God faithfully. Paul was not by any means a beggarly pastor. He was excellent in all scores. Luke was a doctor turned missionary evangelist. He authored the books of Luke and Acts of the Apostles. Philip was an accountant and evangelist whose daughters were mighty prophetesses of the Most High. Levi was a revenue officer while Peter was the owner of Peter & Company Fisheries Enterprises who later turned to be great Fisher of Men (FOM). All these were successful in their fields of endeavour yet they served God meritoriously having God's testimonies over their works.

2. You Cannot Be Rich And Serve God Faithfully?

Some erroneously believe that one cannot be rich and serve God faithfully. To them every Christian who is rich is not right with God. Indeed the opposite is the case. They have deliberately turned the word of God upside down quoting Mark 10:23-25 out of context. Jesus in these verses of the Scripture said:

> *"Then Jesus looked around and said to His disciples, "How hard it is for those who have riches to enter the kingdom of God!" And the disciples were astonished at His words. But Jesus answered again and said to them, "Children, how hard it is for those who trust in riches to enter the kingdom of God! It is easier for a camel to go through the eye of a needle than for a rich man to enter the kingdom of God."*
>
> *(Mark 10:23-25 NKJV)*

The background of this statement was a self acclaimed righteous man came to inquire from Jesus what to do to inherit the kingdom of God. After absolving self from any known sin, Jesus told him the area of his life that must be amended if he hopes to inherit the kingdom of God. Because this man's money was his god, Jesus asked him to go and sell his goods and give to the poor; it was then that his service to God will be accepted. The extent of his love and service to God was revealed after this encounter with Jesus.

For the fact that this man trusted his money and not God he walked away from eternal life. It was not recorded anywhere in the Scriptures that this man came back to God.

It is wrong to take gold and abandon the God who gives the gold but *if you have God He gives you the gold.* Don't be deceived to believe that having riches is the gateway to hell. I wish to state unequivocally this eternal truth that the more of God you serve the more of His money and success you should have. If the opposite is the case with you then there is every need for you to settle down, ask and know why. God does not visit His children with poverty rather He blesses them with good things of life. He said:

> *"I will make all my goodness pass before thee, and I will proclaim the name of the Lord before thee; and will be gracious to whom I will be gracious, and will shew mercy on whom I will shew mercy."*
> *(Exodus 33:19 KJV)*

Poverty is a curse and not a blessing. It is not one of the good and perfect gifts from God.

> *"Every good gift and every perfect gift is from above, and cometh down from the Father of lights, with whom is no variableness, neither shadow of turning."*
>
> *(James 1:17 KJV)*

God's good and perfect gifts are for you because you serve Him.

3. Money Is Evil

This is another fallacy from the pit of hell. Money is no evil. It is the love of money that is the root of all evil. Those who love money and pursue it with unbridled lust and greed only end up with avoidable regrets.

> *"For the love of money is a root of all kinds of evil, for which some have strayed from the faith in their greediness, and pierced themselves through with many sorrows."*
>
> *(1Timothy 6:10 NKJV)*

Deceitfulness of riches thrives in the life ruled by love of money and the resultant effects are darts and pains. Money assumes the character of the holder. If a good man holds money, it is put into good uses. Also if a bad man holds money, it is equally put into wrong uses. So the problem is not with money but with the character of the holder. So when evil and corrupt men hold money they exact negative influence with their possessions and the converse becomes the case when the righteous hold wealth.

4. I can Live Without Money

Your life does not consist of money but you need money for a comfortable living. While on earth you need certain goods and services and money is the common means of exchange for goods and services. With money you may obtain things needed but could not be produced by you. With money you get life necessities and luxuries. With money you get good food, quality clothes and comfortable accommodation. As a matter of fact without money you couldn't have been born, grow and die. At your birth money was necessary to settle the hospital bills, while growing up money plays key role to the quality of life and training given and even at death money is needed for burial expenses.

Even Jesus needed money to pay tax in His days on earth and thus avoided embarrassments from unscrupulous tax officers.

Don't make any mistake about it with money you can do a lot of things and without money you are limited in great number of ways.

5. Money Is For Selected Few

It is possible that many who have tried unsuccessfully to wriggle out of the quagmire of poverty end up with this wrong conclusion that prosperity is for a selected few. "Tell me what next to do that I have not done to be prosperous, someone may say, yet poverty is still trailing me? Therefore, I am destined to be poor while others have the destiny of prosperity. This group of people again is wrong. *God has some favorites when it comes to pouring out His blessings. These are people that obey His principles.* Yes God has principles and those that obey the principles reap bountifully there from.

Jesus was made poor for all men. And the essence was that all men might be rich through His sacrifice on the cross. This was God's general provision for all men in every generation but this provision only works for those who have keyed into it. In *Ecclesiastes 5:9,* God said that *"the profit of the earth is for all."* You are included in "the all." Don't ever try again to exclude yourself from this group of partakers of the prosperity of the Earth. Taking in the poisonous pill that you were destined to be poor drains your energy and hope for a better and prosperous life. It destroys your creative ability. It makes it difficult to believe in God. Thus you should reprogram your mind in line with God's word and this will unleash enormous strength, hope and faith to confront and overcome the hydra headed monster called poverty.

43

Chapter 4

THE REPROACHES OF POVERTY

"..... the destruction of the poor is their poverty." Proverbs 10:15 (NKJV)

Destroy poverty or poverty will destroy you. Stop poverty before poverty stops you. Hate poverty with a cruel passion. Poverty – the state of being without adequate food, clothing, housing, money, etc, is inconceivably repressive and destructive. It is an enigma that has stigmatized and traumatized many individuals, families and nations and should be confronted head long not with self pity and defeatist approach but with concrete determination, smart works and adoption of God given principles. **God says poverty is a destroyer.** He equally said that poverty does not destroy everybody. Poverty destroys only the poor. I cannot put it better. Have you heard that the destruction of the poor is their poverty?

Poverty as much as I know has a beginning and definitely it can be ended. It was not there originally in God's plan for man. It came in as part consequence of man's rebellion against God. The disobedience brought in thorns and thistles. But the good news is that you can decide to overcome and terminate poverty rather than allow poverty to cripple you. Don't remain in the congregation of the dead through ignorance. Common get up! You can wriggle out of the poignant grip of poverty. It is possible!

It is not your fault that you were born poor but it will be your fault if you transit through this world and die poor. You must break free from what used to be by becoming an instrument of change, first to your self, your family and your community. Many families are codified with generational poverty. This poverty is chronic, endemic, and persistent and has run through the family lineages for so long with no one standing up to challenge the status quo. Since the days of old no one in the family has ever risen beyond a certain level and as a result they are ridiculed by others. Here the average mentality and spirit rules. They are denied their due rights and their entire labours amount to no progressive increase.

In all communities the poor have no voice. What a pity! Just like the horns that scattered Israel that none did lift up his head above the set barriers as recorded in Zechariah 1:20, poverty has confined many to unfruitful hard labour. The more they labour, the less they harvest. The benchmark set by poverty elements of ignorance, complacency and lack of focus has become an albatross difficult to destroy.

On a continent wide perspective, poverty is the bane or albatross of mother Africa and has destroyed many dreams and shut down uncountable number of rising stars. The dreams and visions of founding fathers of many African countries of politically and economically free home land still remains a mirage as a result of unconscionable stronghold of poverty perpetrated by bad governance and corruption. How many children of Africa have had their good and strong aspirations shattered and destinies destroyed as a result of inability to wriggle out from the shackles of poverty? How many lives are wasted due to inability to afford treatments from good and workable healthcare systems? How many children of Africa are out of school because of poverty?

Our television tubes everyday showcase the miseries and agonies of poverty. Check out the starving children of Ethiopia! What about Sudan that is devastated and ravaged by the strong and poignant forces of wretchedness, wickedness and unending civil war? You are only left to bewilderments when you see many walking skeletons in Somalia. Poverty is so strong in Somalia yet both the militia and Government spend the limited revenues on arms fighting and killing one another making the country entirely ungovernable. Most of the countries in sub-Saharan Africa have similar miserable tales of poverty and woes to tell. What beats one's imagination is the deplorable state of poverty experienced by many of these countries in the midst of abundant natural endowments and resources.

How about the giant of Africa –Nigeria? The land of liquid gold, the most populous black-country, yet it is estimated that more than eighty percent of her one hundred and fifty million citizens live below the poverty line? This is less than $1 per day. Nigeria is the sixth largest producer of oil in the world yet it is ranked among the poorest in the poverty index. There is no functional infrastructure. The roads are death traps and corruption has eaten the soul of the nation. In the name of political expediencies white is called black among the political class. The masses are so hungry and are crying for help but the leaders are deftly confused feasting on self aggrandizement at the expense of the masses and future of the country.

It is evil and hard to explain that some people in this land of plenty scavenge for livelihood from any thing short of refuse bins. The "humanness" in many of my country men and women are bashed and bastardized by poverty foisted in part by bad leadership, corruption, ignorance, and fear of the unknown and the lack of the will power to boldly step into the future by the common individuals. Some others resort to heinous crimes and social vices as aftermath of being reduced below irreducible minimum by poverty and bankrupt leaders.

Africa is perpetually subjugated to the strangulating holds of the developed world because of poverty and this account for her ever dependence on the West for direction and reliefs. And this will continue until African Leaders decide to end poverty for themselves and their subjects. For *any leader that steals what he holds in trust for his people for selfish reasons is bereft of understanding.* Though before men he appears affluent but in reality and deep within him, he is poorer than the poorest of the land.

In life the rich rule the poor and the debtor will always serve the creditor. There is nothing any one can do to change this law. Africa for example is ruled by the developed World either covertly or overtly. This may sound controversial or appear topical which is not intended but with every sense of humility and modesty let's answer this question: Yea, some of Africa are free politically but are they truly free economically? I don't think so. Do most of these African countries depend on the developed world perennially for aids and grants and possible debt forgiveness or relief? Nigeria just got one from her foreign creditors! And after that due to poor management the nation is gradually drifting into the odd path of debt thereby mortgaging the welfare of future generations. This will continue as long as some of our leaders keep plundering and impoverishing themselves and the land by stealing what they don't even need to survive.

The rich exact controlling authority over the poor. The Bible says:

> *"The rich rule over the poor, and the borrower is servant to the lender. (Proverbs 22:7 NIV)*

This is an eternal and spiritual law that cannot be altered or changed. The rich think on how to consolidate and keep on increasing while the poor think and take actions that subjugate them further into poverty. The only way for you not to be ruled and ridiculed is to be genuinely rich. You are at the mercy of whosoever that feeds you and that is why we have many sycophants in our country today engaging in acts they would not ordinarily take part in with their sane minds.

Every creditor sets the rules for borrowing. You don't borrow based on your terms. The borrowing conditions are spelt out by the lender. And the money is made available to only those that meet the conditions set by the lender. The lender calls the shots. He collects the principal, interests, fees and punitive default charges which is at terrible cost to the borrower. The creditor is entitled to call in his funds from the borrower at any given time. That is why the debtor is servant to the creditor.

There are many people who have prospered genuinely in the land. Thank God for them and may their days be long. But there are few who have spoiled and plundered the land and wants to intimidate, dominate and subjugate every other person in penury by all means. But I see an emerging class whose increase is not by in-dignifying demeanor of stealing and corruption but by complete obedience to God's financial principles of honesty and smart works. These are generations of liberators that will free their households, communities and the nation from the destructive strands of poverty.

Poverty from the foregoing is no respecter of sex, religion, colour or age. It is ready to embarrass and destroy you if you fail to deal with it frontally.

The Man Of God Who Died a Debtor

In the Bible there was a "whole" man of God who died a debtor. This man had a testimony of fearing the Lord but unfortunately he died without appreciating and appropriating the enormity of God's abundance. His story epitomizes the debilitating consequences of poverty that inevitably never ended with him. The entire family was enslaved to poverty by his borrowings. Though the family may have loved him but he bequeathed on them legacy of heart break, pains and shame. Those that never knew when the debt agreement was struck got to know that the family was in serious debt crisis because poverty impaired the man's ability to repay and the creditors had no option than to call in the collateral. And guess what the collateral was? The prophet's two sons!

> *"Now there cried a certain woman of the wives of the sons of the prophets unto Elisha, saying, Thy servant my husband is dead; and thou knowest that thy servant did fear the Lord: and the creditor is come to take unto him my two sons to be bondmen.*
>
> *And Elisha said unto her, what shall I do for thee? Tell me, what hast thou in the house? And she said thine handmaid hath not any thing in the house, save a pot of oil. Then he said, go, borrow thee vessels abroad of all thy neighbours, even empty vessels; borrow not a few. And when thou art come in, thou shalt shut the door upon thee and upon thy sons, and shalt pour out into all those vessels, and thou shalt set aside that which is full. So she went from him, and shut the door upon her and upon her sons, who brought the vessels to her; and she poured out. And it came to pass, when the vessels were full, that she said unto her son, bring me yet a vessel. And he said unto her, there is not a vessel more. And the oil stayed. Then she came and told the man of God. And he said, Go, sell the*

oil, and pay thy debt, and live thou and thy children of the rest".
(2 Kings 4:1-7 KJV)

This man of God in question died a pauper leaving unbearable debt burden on the helpless wife and two sons now positioned for enslavement due to their father's debts. To the woman the agony of widowhood was painful but the strain of losing the sons to the creditor was more humiliating and crushing.

The widow did something beyond crying that ended the yoke of poverty. Do something now to destroy the choking yoke of poverty! The widow turned to God who the husband served but never believed enough to end his financial predicaments. The result was amazing. *By simple act of faith on the word of God abundance emanated through a little pot of oil and the strong shackles of poverty over that family were broken. Was the oil not there all these while? The difference was the power of God on the oil.*

Prior to this encounter with the man of God it remained ordinary oil but after the encounter it assumed another divinely ordained role of channel of increase and abundance. The consequential disgrace of the debt burden imposed on this family was banished. The creditors were repaid and the family had a new understanding of God's workings. Fear, crying and sleepless nights were rolled away. Joy and family union that was under threat were restored and a new chapter of prosperity was opened for the entire family.

I want to believe the children began to see God as caring and not as one who is not in a position to provide for those who serve Him. Don't allow your children or the unbelieving question the God you serve as a result of humiliating blows of poverty. Arise in faith out of the ridicule of poverty. Arise for you can make it and don't allow the reproaches of poverty to continue.

Chapter 5

ASHES TO BEAUTY

"To appoint unto them that mourn in Zion, to give unto them beauty for ashes...."

(Isaiah 61:3)

You may not have had the best of background due to incidence of birth. Every thing around you now may be pointing to direction of failure and poverty. It may equally appear that the more you struggle with life realities to wriggle out of present quagmire of poverty the more you are enmeshed in it. Don't give up hope for your time of extrication from poverty and frustration is here.

Many as you are had very poor and little beginning but never allowed the limitations inherent in their circumstances to stop them from becoming the best they could be in life.

Probably you were born into an unenviable family! Possibly with wooden spoons and it appears you were condemned to poverty by incidence of birth. That is not the end of your story. The better side of life is coming your way. The best of your life story is yet to be told. *Posterity will not judge you for being born into a poor family but will not be kind with you if you fail to rise above defeatist tendencies to cause a change in your life time.*

Silver spoon or wooden spoon does not really matter. This may have affected your smooth head start in life but they are not strong enough to derail your life purpose. The equation of life is turning to your own good. What matters is what you make out of who you are and what you have. What matters is that you have a great future ahead of you. What is important is that you can start to do something that will trigger chain of changes to translate you from ashes to beauty. What matters is what God says concerning you and what you make out of it. Wrong opinions or misjudgments of people about you and unfavourable circumstances of life are not as important as what you make out of them.

David was an unrecognized poor shepherd lad from an unknown family but out of obscurity he rose to become second king of Israel. You can make it. Jesus don't forget was born in a manger but this never limited his person.

I am a living witness of those that God changed their status. He exchanged my poverty for His riches and I am glad to testify about it all the time. I will devote the rest of this chapter to tell you a little of my life story. I had a little beginning that ordinarily placed some constraint on my life ladder. I never allowed this to deter or destroy me. I decided to concentrate on the positive side of life and I am moving up.

Despite the poor and little beginning, the pains and hard knocks of life trainings, my parents were supportive and caring and sacrificed all to give me and my siblings the best they could afford. And I sincerely praise God for giving me such parents that gave me hope and assurance and the tenacity to press along. They were simply the best parents any could have who never allowed us to bemoan the then difficult but temporary moments but were persistently unwavering in training us to believe in God, to believe in self, to live an honest and innocuous life while expecting better tomorrow. They sacrificed indeed for us to have a better tomorrow.

There was a time in my life that we ate rice only once in long while. There was a time in my life that I wore new cloth only once in a year and that was on Christmas day. But all that is history now because I have been translated from ashes to beauty.

Your background can but should not limit you from rising from failure to true success, from the ashes of poverty, disdain and ridicule to the stairways of riches- stairways of riches because riches are in stages and progressive. All of us have different events impacting our lives. Most of these events are beyond our control but our response to theses events are within our control. *The events that dot your life and your response to them determine the outcome(s) you get.*

Looking back at my past, everything and almost everybody except God said I was going to be a failure. Someone even told me when I was about fourteen years old that I will amount to nothing if ever trained. But how wrong he was? Indeed, I had a poor and humble background. I am really proud of my little beginning. No regrets about that! It has made me to prove that God lifts up from the dungeon.

I am from a polygamous family and I and seven of my siblings were the children of my father's old age. Ordinarily in the context of African family culture from our placement in the family linage, surrounded by big brothers and sisters, uncles and aunties who were by no means renowned and people of substance in their own rights, we were supposed to have the best for arriving on the stage at the time we did, but that was not to be.

My parents got married after my father retired from the services of the Nigeria Railway Corporation in early 1960's. My mother was the last among four wives and it was not really easy for her being the last of four wives in a polygamous home though loved by my father. By order of birth, I am the fourth son of my father but the third child of my mother and her first son. Born in the midst of the Nigeria civil war, I survived against all odds of kwashiorkor, abandonment and persistent but sporadic exchange of gun fires that lasted for about three years. Many children born during the civil war were either killed by enemy fire power or by the effects of the war. Many children were inadvertently abandoned by the parents during the war. Many thanks to my mother for not abandoning me but carried me on her back when running from the then enemy forces.

My father's older three sons and six daughters were from his other two wives. My father believed in human capital development. Thus he spent most of his life earnings and resources training his first generation children, brothers, cousins and impacted positively many immediate and distant relations while he had the means. By the time we came on stage everything was almost dry. Unfortunately, these human capital investments as it relates to his older sons never really paid off as disasters struck in the family three times along the way through cold hands of death within a space of five years. Sadly and prematurely too, my father's second son was killed during the Nigeria civil war. I never knew him. The third son who was working in a bank in Enugu the then capital of East Central State of Nigeria died in 1970 through a ghastly motor accident while returning to his base at Enugu after a short holiday and the first son died in 1974.

As a result of these harrowing experiences, my father was literally called in my place, the "Job" of our time. Though my father was broken by these sad happenings, yet he was not destroyed. He simply forged ahead. In the midst of these sad developments, the Lord found my father and through the encounter with the Lord, I and my siblings got to have a personal relationship with the Lord. The entire family indeed became the converts and first fruit of my father's conversion to the Lord

Encounters with the Lord set us on a different pedestal and opened the floodgates of hope, persistence and survival in life endeavours. My father always said "I never bequeathed estates and wealth to you but I have betrothed you to JESUS who is greater than riches." Thus I embraced the Lord from a tender age of seven and this early encounter and relationship with the Lord Jesus Christ greatly shaped who I am today.

My father never went past standard two in those days, though he could read and write and he had passion for education. He once said that "position pass power." He believes education serves as a launching pad for better positioning. And once you are in position you stand to utilize the power therein. But to what use you put the power depends on you.

For me passing through the primary and secondary schools was really hard and rough. *Well every stage in life is a phase. That you are a labourer today does not mean you will not be an employer of labour*

tomorrow. The burden of raising my siblings and I rested on my mother and aging father. Both were involved in subsistence farming. My father's menial pension trickled in infrequently. As a matter of fact the Nigeria Railway Corporation owed him over thirty six months pension arrears at the time of his death in February 1999. The entire family was involved at various times in assorted menial labour works just to earn some income to augment our up keep and trainings.

There was really no hope humanly speaking for any one of my mother's children advancing to or beyond the Secondary school. The condition was critical and when it appeared I was going to drop from school especially towards the tail end of my primary education up to my second year in the secondary school a paternal auntie played some intervening roles and ensured that I continued my education. My auntie (fondly called my second mother); the husband and the entire family greatly accommodated and graciously paid my school fees for about four years and this intervention kept hope of advancement in school alive.

I was not disappointing in my school works. I finished the primary school on a high note, graduating with distinction in the First School Leaving Certificate in 1980. The only one in the school that year! I also gained admission to the secondary school the same year.

From the time I left leaving with my auntie, every time school was in session I rode bicycle to and from secondary school which is tens of kilometers from my village. Most times I stayed back in school till around five o'clock in the evening reading when most of my colleagues had gone home. This studious expedition paid off handsomely. Apart from first term class two that I came third in the examinations, I took the first position in all other classes from class one to class five.

I obtained the West African School Certificate in 1985 graduating with the best result in my Secondary School (Nekede Boy's Secondary School, Owerri, Imo State) that year. It was a celebrated result also in my little village of Amaeze, Owerri. At least the result earned me some respect and recognition! This feat seemed to be the end of the road but it was actually the very beginning of another journey. While the direction for what lies ahead seemed hazy I was preoccupied with Christian religious activities and exercises building my faith in the Lord. I was actively engaged in evangelism, prayers and bible studies.

In 1987, I left the village to Lagos to stay with my senior sister and her family. This gave a new lease of life. I had passion to study either of three courses namely, medicine, finance or journalism. Medicine was first in the pecking order followed by finance. But there were strong limitations to my studying medicine. Aside from having longer years than reading finance the cost of reading medicine was equally higher. Thus I decided to aim at what was cheaper and shorter.

I was employed in 1988 on contract basis as a clerk in American International Insurance Company, now AIICO Insurance Plc-one of the leading insurance companies in the country. My start up contract wages was one hundred and fifty naira (₦150), about one dollar ($1) per month in today's value. After three months I was given full employment. Then I was in the disbursement section, writing claims cheques and carrying out other duties assigned to me by my supervisor. I was really diligent, humble, tenacious and observant.

Working in that insurance company broadened my horizon and perspective in life. I watched diligently as the days and months passed bye the agony and bitter complaints of some of those who had been in the employment of the company for years over how their emoluments were not enough for them. These complaints I have come to know were peculiar with most employees. Many complained always that their take home could not take them home. Management was always unfair whenever it comes to staff welfare was the general impression. To some of them there was nothing inspiring on the job –they were only wasting away, yet they got glued only because of the monthly salaries, no better alternatives and the fear of taking their destinies in their hands by resigning to new ventures. Some had been employed for upward of ten years and there seemed to be no silver lining in the sky. They could not quit but it was obvious they were not enjoying what they were doing. Unfortunately many were laid off in no time during right sizing exercise carried out by the company and the fear they refused to confront hit them headlong.

One day, as I sat back in the office various thoughts were flashing through my head. I thought if some of these people had been in this company for all these years and there is to me nothing to show for it (evidently from the complaints and life styles of some of them), what will be my fate if I continue like this group of people without seeking for self improvements?

Now they are earning higher salaries than my self and yet what I hear are tales of discontentment; will I not be on the same path if I only have to depend on salary enhancement without self improvements or developments? I did some soul searching and self evaluation of what I wanted. I calculated if I continued on this present salary scale, what will be my worth in the next five years? Who will bear the cost of my education since I desired to go to University? If my present salary is kept constant or even if there is a raise every year by a certain percentage, will this be enough to take care of myself, my aging parents and train my other siblings and still meet up with other undefined commitments? What will life be like if I marry at this present salary scale? Will I be able to take care of my wife and the children that follow while in this employment without self improvement? What about my obligations in the Church and Society?

I became obsessed with the thoughts for change and what the future holds. And this made me restive and set me apart to reason outside the confinements of the circumstances that surrounded me. I was largely driven by search for pleasures beyond the pains confronting me.

Even without the faintest hope of any sponsorship, I bought the University Matriculations Examination entry form in 1989. When I was offered a provisional admission to read Banking and Finance in University of Port Harcourt, Rivers State, Nigeria the offer was mixed simultaneously with happiness and sadness. Happiness because I had long desired to go to the University and now the opportunity is right before me and sadness because there were no defined and assured sources to finance my University training and the odds that this admission opportunity may be lost were really high.

By the time the University admission offer letter came, I had a total savings of about five hundred naira (₦500), less than $4. I took permission from the office and traveled to the school and registered for the academic session. The school was bubbling and bustling with life and all manner of exuberances. I was thrilled that at last I have stepped into a citadel of learning as a student. A window of self improvement is right before me. This relieved the temporary sadness and burden of no sponsorship. However, the sadness aggravated when I returned back to Lagos when it clearly dawned on me that there was no definite source of sponsorship for my University education and that I may not be going back to the school after all to commence studies.

There were three schools of thought on the way forward. One was that I should defer the University admission for one year, that is, not to resign from the present employment and devote the next year working including overtime on both Saturdays and Sundays just to accumulate some savings before going to school. But this thought was fraught with great limitations. If I had worked for a little over two years without gathering enough savings, how much will I earn and save in the next year that will be enough to see me through school for the four years duration of the course? Even if I save some money to get to school, what happens when the savings are exhausted? Will I seek to defer the schooling and get back to work to earn some money and then go back to school? Will the job be there waiting for me?

The second school of thought was to forgo the admission entirely and enroll for a part time degree program with University of Lagos. This option was inconceivably retrogressive because the admission conditions then were just out of reach. (In late 80's to early 90's there were few Universities offering part time courses for undergraduates in Nigeria). The two principal conditions precedent to gaining admission in University of Lagos part time degree programme then were that each applicant must not be less than thirty five years of age and the applicant must have had ten years cognate work experience. At this stage in my life I was just twenty two years old. I wondered in disillusionment into the distant future how I will be wasting and waiting for the next thirteen years to be qualified to enroll in the part time degree program. What if there are intervening variables that will alter the focus and drive for better tomorrow before I am thirty five years? This to me was not an option to consider.

When it seemed that there was no plausible means out of the dilemma, I decided against all odds and sensibilities to resign from my office and headed to the school which was the third option that actually never made sense anyway to many. In fact it was stupid to resign from work to head to school when you were not sure of how you will be trained. But the stupidity paid off. I remember telling one of my friends back then when I was leaving to the University that I was embarking on a suicide mission. To me it was better to resign and head to school even without known sponsor than to waste and rot in a job and poverty stigmatization that inhibit my rising to the next level of life and never gave me comfort and satisfaction.

But God was there for me. He is equally here now with you. In fact God went ahead of me. I remember when I informed my then Pastor, Reverend Henry Ogbonnaya of the University admission and my resignations from office and from the post of the Youth President of my local Church, Assemblies of God, Agboju, Lagos, Nigeria, he gave an inspired message that lives with me till today. He said; "the faith in you is enough to see you through." How right this inspired message turned to be! I was fired up in the midst of uncertainties.

When I got to the University, I embarked on three days praying and fasting, seeking God's guidance and intervention in my affairs. At the end of the fast, that beautiful cool evening, I was walking back from where we called in those days in University of Port Harcourt wailing garden (this was the University's Botanical garden used by Christians for prayers. Hardly was there any time that no one was praying in that garden whether in the day and or night. I have no doubt that fruits of the tireless prayers of the saints in that University are abounding), I heard the voice of the Lord with a message that kept and sustained me all through my stay in School. The Lord said, *"Son when you were coming to this School you said you were embarking on a suicide mission but today I have changed that 'suicide mission' to 'providence mission'."* You see God was there when I determined to launch into the open sea rather than stay back in the confines of limitations. He was there when I launched out to the uncharted sea in faith. God was listening when I told my friend that it's better to move forward in this 'suicide mission' than to be static and still perish. This was the turning point. God over ruled all the fears, uncertainties and limitations that stared at me and kept His word by sustaining me all through my sojourning in the University.

God's ways are mysterious and wondrous! He went ahead and moved my nephew (the son of my father's first son) who lives in United States of America who became an instrument in underwriting most of my bills in the School. This God-sent nephew came to the stage when there was no hope and the help was most needed even when it was not compelling, obligatory or compulsory on him to give a helping hand to me. Apart from the monetary support provided he was always advising me to be forthright, diligent and never give in to the ills bedeviling the society and sinking many youths. To this my caring nephew I am indebted and sincerely grateful. God equally raised others who ordinarily should have nothing to do with augmenting my school bills to come in at each point of need to ensure that I graduated without letting finances pose any serious hindrance.

I recall one of the incidences that happened in my final year that could have spelt disaster to my graduating from the school. I had only one semester away from becoming a graduate and lo it appeared that this dream was not going to be after all. I lost the whole money given to me by my nephew for my second semester up keeps and project works to fraudsters. It was as though the end had come and I wasn't going to brace the tape at last. I was afraid to write to him in far away United States of America. I could not even tell my aged parents till after my graduation for fear of suffering heart attacks. But help came from unusual quarters in bits. When I left Lagos back to school on resumption I left with one thousand naira (₦1,000) dashed to me by a Christian brother who learnt that I fell victim to fraudsters. Truly how I managed to survive those harrowing last four months of my undergraduate days is still a wonder to me.

How miraculous are your works oh God! God raised men who helped me and He will do same for you. *If God has placed you in a position to assist others, do it willingly because if you refuse you may never have the opportunity to be part of God's workings in those lives again.* Your obedient sacrifice today in helping someone in need may release a chain of reactions tomorrow that will impact or change many lives for good.

I am not lazy academically, vocationally and spiritually. Each holiday period, I always ran back to Lagos for vacation jobs. AIICO Insurance Plc was equally helpful in providing the space for me for vacation job. The sail was windy, bumpy and stormy but all the same I landed safely with a Bachelor of Science Degree, Second Class Honours, Upper Division in Banking and Finance. To date I have a Masters Degree in Business Administration; I am Chartered Banker and a full Manager leading a branch in a new generation Bank in Nigeria which in the wildest imagination of many was not to be years back. And I know that this is just the beginning.

Have I arrived? Emphatic no is the answer. The scripture says in *1 Corinthians 8:2-3 "and if anyone thinks that he knows anything, he knows nothing yet as he ought to know." (NKJV)*

You can apply this scripture to every area of life. If you think you are something, forget it you are nothing yet. Whatever you have and are is nothing compared to what you ought to have and be. Thus there is only one acceptable way to go. Upward! I am just beginning. I still have great mileages and milestones before me. I am pregnant with great dreams. As I consistently work with God and diligently apply myself in the course of life I know there will not be any deliberate miscarriages of my dreams. And by the grace of God, I shall not come down to the levels I have crossed. I must influence lives by impacting positively this generation to the glory of God. The extent of the success is actually going to be measured by the number of people I affect for good and not necessarily the volume of money amassed.

I have taken out time to tell you a bit of my journey from ashes to beauty. It may not have made an interesting reading but the thrust of the story is that you should not allow your low beginning or any event of life to stop you from moving forward. The incidence of birth and circumstances that surrounded my upbringing could have grounded me if I had allowed them. But that was not to be. The thought of having no one to assuredly lean on for my University trainings was enough choking pain but instead of destroying me it became a propelling force to move me ahead in life. I was afraid of being a failure to self, my parents and dependent relatives. This fear never drowned me but pushed me to drive for change.

Your situation may even be worst or precarious than I experienced. Yet nothing on the outside of you has the potency to stop you from becoming great and freed from the shackles of poverty and under fulfillment.

I had a desire for a better tomorrow and to be a channel of help to others. I never wanted to end up tapping palm wine in the village. Not that tapping palm wine is a bad occupation and I don't mean to be ludicrous but such menial job is synonymous to failure and associated with old and fading men. I never wanted to be a worthless son who could not contribute to the betterment of his parents and other dependent relatives. My father am sure before he went to be with the Lord in 1999 at the ripe age of one hundred and ten was happy with who I was then and how happier he would be if the Lord gives him the privilege of knowing what I am now and will be tomorrow. To my mother who the Lord sustained during those years of hardship, sufferings and pains, I have not been a disappointment. In fact, she is reaping in parts of the fruits of her audacious sacrifice.

The secret was that I did what was humanly possible and believed in God for what was divinely possible. I did not brood over things I could not possibly change and begrudge those I thought could have helped me but didn't after all in vain is salvation hoped from hills and mountains; salvation is only from the Lord. By the grace of God I am impacting some lives positively today. I am waxing stronger in faith. I have trained five people already in the tertiary institutions and more will follow and presently I and my family are actively involved in some charity activities helping the needy in our little ways.

Like everyone else you may have good reasons to fail. But no matter how strong and cogent the excuses may sound, they are not strong enough to stop you from advancing forward out of the woods of penury and rejection. *Most great men were born small. But rather than be limited by their little beginning this serves as the driving force to greatness.* Have a desire, be focused and be passionate for success. Your expectation cannot be cut off. Then you've got to back up your determination to succeed with right and timely actions and you will be shocked that nothing on the outside is strong enough to stop you from prospering in life.

My guiding principle has ever been: Is God in this? What has God said about the issue?

And once I am convinced that God is in it, and I have an understanding of what His word says on a particular issue, I will stick out my neck regardless of the odds. And He has not failed me in any way and He will not change in your own case.

Are you presently wearing rags of failure, rejection and poverty? Come on this is not the end of the story. The best of your story is still ahead. Rise up from the ashes of despondency; mix your hope for better tomorrow with right actions. Dust your self up and get moving for things that are ahead of you are far greater in value than the frustrations of today or failed dreams of yesterday. *Be not complacent. This can suffocate your tomorrow.* Rather be discontent with the present ugly circumstances, yearn for change and do something positively. *Learn also to challenge the status quo if you must experience change.* Tomorrow for sure shall be better than today if only you do something positive today. God is with you and you shall be clothed with beauty. Don't despair but trust in God who only can turn your sorrow to joy; your darkness to light and your failure to success. He is not tired of you and is very pathetic of your sufferings. Be sure He is coming for you to change your garment from ashes to beauty. He did it for me and sure will do same for you.

Chapter 6

MENTAL REORIENTATION

"For as he thinketh in his heart, so is he:" (Proverbs 23:7)

Slavery Mentality

It all begins in the mind. If you are poor in your mind, you will be poor in your thoughts, actions and attendant outputs. If you have a bankrupt, twisted and polluted mind what you produce will not be different either. What you are on the inside automatically reflects in your thoughts, attitude, words, actions, and results. Indeed your words and actions sum up what obtains on your inside. *"For out of the abundance of the heart the mouth speaketh." (Matthew 12:34 KJV)*

If you are held in bondage by wrong and poor mental inclinations and deductions, outside greatness will be very far from you. You cannot rise above your thoughts. If the eyes of your mind are blind you will stumble in the daylight. Jesus said *"If therefore the light that is in thee be darkness, how great is that darkness! (Matthew 6:23 KJV)*

Wrong information leads to wrong mindsets, actions and results. This was part of the problem that most of the children of Israel had after the triumphant exit from Egypt. They allowed the tortuous circumstances of slavery in Egypt to precondition their minds. *The people of a BIG GOD who witnessed supernatural visitations and deliverances in Egypt soon after leaving the land of bondage and cruelty began to limit the Omnipotent God in the figments of their small minds. Their fickle minds could not comprehend the capability and availability of God.*

Israel was physically out of Egypt but many of their minds were still patterned after Egypt. This was very often demonstrated by their words and actions. Most of them vehemently refused to renew their minds in line with God's gracious provisions. And as a result of the mind block they saw and acted as slaves. Each time they lost the battle in their minds, the consequences were usually disastrous. Their wrong mental inclinations were diametrically opposed to what God can do.

At each time they tried to stone Moses for not leading in their own ways, they had thought that already in their minds. Indeed their action was a mere manifestation of what was in their minds.

Before they murmured and complained out loudly, this has already taken root in their minds. Before they went a-whoring, they had attempted that severally in their minds.

Before they tried to go back to Egypt, the battle was already fought and lost in their minds. Each time they complained and murmured for either food or water in the wilderness, they had already concluded in their minds that God was not able again to fix the problems.

Equally before they declared themselves grasshoppers, they had already visualized in their minds how they were eaten up by the giants in the land. And what they saw was what they got.

One People, Same Conditions but Different Attitudes:

Recall all the children of Israel were slaves in the land of Egypt for four hundred and thirty years. They served under same conditions of oppression, harassment, intimidation, marginalization, frustration and denials. They had the same history and heritage. Whilst in Egypt slavery mentality robbed off on all of them. They were subjugated to all kinds of deprivations and unimaginable dehumanizing conditions. Their due wages were denied them by their Egyptian task masters. In fact their debasement was terrible that at a point all male children of Israeli parentage were sentenced to death even before birth and make no mistake about it enforcers were sent out by the Egyptian authorities to execute this ungodly and inhumane decree. It was during this trying time that Moses was born yet he rose to become great. What an inauspicious time for one to be born! ***Your birth and circumstances are not accidental to God. There is a purpose for coming to the stage the time you did.***

On the night of Israel's departure from Egypt God manifested and handsomely rewarded them. After perfuming Israel with favour, He commanded them to go receive gold, silver and precious jewels from their oppressive Egyptian neighbours. This is how God is transferring wealth from those who do not know and serve Him to those who love Him. Get into the flow.

> *"And I will make the Egyptians favorably disposed toward this people, so that when you leave you will not go empty-handed. Every woman is to ask her neighbor and any woman living in her house for articles of silver and gold and for clothing, which you will put on your sons and daughters. And so you will plunder the Egyptians."*
>
> *(Exodus 3:21-22 NIV)*
>
> *"The LORD had made the Egyptians favorably disposed toward the people, and they gave them what they asked for; so they plundered the Egyptians." (Exodus 12:36 NIV)*

It is imperative we make the point that God had to reward Israel for four hundred and thirty years of impoverishment, subservient treatments and unpaid labours suffered in the hands of the Egyptian slave masters for the following reasons:

First, a worker is worthy of his wages. It is wickedness when you fail to pay your workers their wages. This can attract the wrath of God.

> *"...for the labourer is worthy of his hire." (Luke 10:7 KJV)*
>
> *"Woe unto him that buildeth his house by unrighteousness, and his chambers by wrong; that useth his neighbour's service without wages, and giveth him not for his work;" (Jeremiah 22:13 KJV)*

Though Egypt was determined not to send Israel away or at the very least send them away empty handed, God who did not call us to serve Him in vain had to intervene and marvelously compensated

Israel. ***In fact it is a curse to exploit someone's labour without pay.*** I declare unto you by the Lord that all your years of unpaid labour have been released to you. It does not matter the hands holding forth, now is your time of recompense and every stronghold is falling apart by the power of the Almighty God. God did it yesterday and He will do it again today for *"Jesus Christ is the same yesterday, today and forever." (Hebrews 13:8 KJV)*

Second, **God before placing any demand on us makes the provisions.** He provided the gold, silver, precious jewels, raiment, etc, because of the demand to be placed on the children of Israel in the wilderness. There was going to be a need to build Tabernacle of Congregation in the wilderness, thus God made the provisions ahead of time. Let it be said again that God will before every demand make the provisions it is then left to the willing hearted to respond in love by giving out of what He has provided.

Despite the fact that God graciously rewarded the children of Israel the concern is how come people with similar background; that had awesome divine visitations; confronted with same challenges and opportunities came off with mixed results? Some came through to be rich while others were satisfied being poor!

> *"The LORD your God has blessed you in all the work of your hands. He has watched over your journey through this vast desert. These forty years the LORD your God has been with you, and you have not lacked anything. (Deuteronomy 2:7 NIV)*

1. The children of Israel savoured the same grace in the wilderness.

2. Manna and meat was released to them for the forty years they wandered in the wilderness. They lacked absolutely nothing.

3. They all abode under divine covering of pillar of cloud and fire in the day and night respectively. Thanks for this awesome presence of Jehovah!

4. None of them also was feeble nor had swollen foot for the forty years of sojourning in the desert. Even the old among them had strength of the youth. Caleb at eighty five years

declared he had the strength of a forty year old man. Moses was one hundred and twenty years with undiminished vigour. He died a strong man.

5. ***The people of Israel walked into ripe harvest in the land of Canaan. The same day they stepped into this harvest, manna ceased falling from Heaven for all of them.***

All of Israel entered the land of Canaan at the same time and were confronted with the same challenges and opportunities. But how come that some of these people that faced similar circumstances and opportunities in the course of years advanced to be superfluously wealthy while many found solace in abject poverty?

The answer was what happened in their individual minds defined their response to God's words. It also defined how they responded to challenges and opportunities. Those that lost the battle of the mind lost the battle of the land. Those that refused to walk away from their old shadow or nature of mental slavery were distressed but all that renewed their minds through God's laws, abundance and peace of mind became their lot. ***The battle of the mind is very central to winning the battle of poverty in particular and life in general.***

There should be no poor among you

To God being poor is not the perfect state for man. It is only a conditional or transitional state.

> *"However, there should be no poor among you, for in the land the LORD your God is giving you to possess as your inheritance, he will richly bless you, if only you fully obey the LORD your God and are careful to follow all these commands I am giving you today. For the LORD your God will bless you as he has promised, and you will lend to many nations but will borrow from none. You will rule over many nations but none will rule over you. If there is a poor man among your brothers in any of the towns of the land that the LORD your God is giving you, do not be hardhearted or tightfisted toward your poor brother. Rather be openhanded and freely lend him whatever he needs. Be careful not to harbor this wicked thought: "The seventh year, the year for canceling debts, is*

near," so that you do not show ill will toward your needy brother and give him nothing. He may then appeal to the LORD against you, and you will be found guilty of sin. Give generously to him and do so without a grudging heart; then because of this the LORD your God will bless you in all your work and in everything you put your hand to. There will always be poor people in the land. Therefore I command you to be openhanded toward your brothers and toward the poor and needy in your land." (Deuteronomy 15:4-8 NIV)

God's cardinal stance on poverty is that there should be no poor in the land (verse 4). But because He knew that many will not imbibe and appropriate His principles on riches He stated in verse 7 of Deuteronomy chapter 15, that "if there is a poor man among your brothers....." This was a conditional statement dependent on what we make out of His Word which outlines the principles of riches and well being. But the points we want to note are:

1. All Israel that came out of Egypt had eyes beholding same lands, conditions, environment, and enemies but they saw differently. While some saw giants, insurmountable mountains and problems, others saw opportunities for greatness.

2. There were various and different interpretations to what they saw. And the extent of their vision and interpretation determined how far each individual could go. What each one saw on the inside determined the visible results obtained.

3. Over the years, two classes of people emerged from the people of Israel that came out from Egypt – the rich and strong and the poor and weak.

4. What each man became financially was as a result of his attitude towards God's financial principles.

5. The poor were always on the borrowing or begging side of life while the rich were commanded to be open handed in giving to the poor.

God laid it bare that there will be the rich and the poor in the land.

Not because He wanted it that way, not because that is the best but because some may choose to be poor by thought and action. Thus, two people with different mind sets looking at this portion of the Scripture may choose to react in two dissimilar ways.

The Man with Rich Mentality

The man with rich mentality among the children of Israel obviously will think this way:

What must I do to be rich since this state is possible and attainable given that all of us are exposed to the same conditions and opportunities with no one having a competitive advantage? Do I really wish to end up begging for a living? I want to have in order to give! So what must I do to have? What problems can I provide solutions for?

The man will sit back tasking his brain, searching for information on business opportunities and seeking counsel on God's financial principles and improving his God given talents by doing. Because he has positive inclination towards riches, he sets out to learn the dynamics of riches and with time his actions, words and associations begin to attract what his mind has attuned to on the inside. His mind yearns for increase because he has prosperity possibility mentality. The mind longs for prosperity eliciting positive actions. ***Whenever the mind cries for change (prosperity); actions demonstrate this and result obtained is only a confirmation.***

The Man with Poverty Mentality

This man is contented to note that there will always be the poor in the land. After all he will say I am not the only poor man in the land. That is his consolation. The man with poverty stricken mentality takes this portion of the Scripture out of context that since God said that there will be the rich and the poor in the land, it means that he is among those destined to be poor. So let's take what fate brings to us. He will blame every other person but himself for his poor condition and never takes consistent positive actions for change.

Truly this man is poor on the inside and same manifests on the outside. The mind is twisted towards riches thus when he sees challenges, they stand as problems instead of opportunities to increase. He fails to realize that *you are paid proportionately to the magnitude of problems you are able to solve.*

You Are What You Think

"For as he thinks in his heart, so is he." (Proverbs 23:7 NKJV)

The label you wear is a manifestation of what you are on the inside. You are what you think. Your actions cannot be separated from how and what you think. If you are filled with poverty thoughts; disappointment, sorrow and poverty is what you will attract. Conversely, if your thoughts are noble, you will equally attract noble things. Many who are coerced to confess that they like riches, good things of life without inward convictions only end up with actions that negate their confessions. This is because the right information is not fed on the mind. And thus after many long confessions and without change they are still where they were confused and frustrated. If deep in your mind you believe that riches is made for selected or anointed few which you are not included no matter how long you confess that prosperity is yours because you are Abraham's seed you will still be far away from the gates of riches. You can not attract what you hate.

God enjoins us to develop the habit of thinking excellent thoughts.

"Finally, brothers, whatever is true, whatever is noble, whatever is right, whatever is pure, whatever is lovely, whatever is admirable- if anything is excellent or praiseworthy-think about such things." (Philippians 4:8 NIV)

As a child of God you are prohibited from thinking any thing outside these boundaries of thought set out by God in the Scripture above. Don't allow the devil destroy you with perverse thoughts. Your thinking pattern affects your value judgment, your actions and what you get.

Grasshopper Mentality

Let's stress more on this point of thinking true inside out with the

Scriptural illustration below. The children of Israel were moments away from entering into the Promised Land when Moses selected twelve leaders to search through the land with the following mandate:

> *"When Moses sent them to explore Canaan, he said, "Go up through the Negev and on into the hill country. See what the land is like and whether the people who live there are strong or weak, few or many. What kind of land do they live in? Is it good or bad? What kind of towns do they live in? Are they unwalled or fortified? How is the soil? Is it fertile or poor? Are there trees on it or not? Do your best to bring back some of the fruit of the land." (It was the season for the first ripe grapes.) (Numbers 13:17-20 NIV)*

At the end of forty days the leaders came back with two different reports –the majority and the minority reports. The report of the majority was voluminous yet the contents were not in sync and diametrically opposite to the purpose of God for Israel. ***And once your focus and pursuit in life is not in line with God's purpose undesirable end will always result.*** If it is in today's parlance, the minority report would have been branded dissenting voice. And the conclusion would be, "let the minority have their say and the majority have their way." That's the beauty of democracy but that's not with God. The minority that opts to stand with God will have their way for he that is with God is majority. Lets us consider the results in detail.

Majority Report (83%)

> *"They gave Moses this account: "We went into the land to which you sent us, and it does flow with milk and honey! Here is its fruit. But the people who live there are powerful and the cities are fortified and very large. We even saw descendants of Anak there. The Amalekites live in the Negev; the Hittites, Jebusites and Amorites live in the hill country; and the Canaanites live near the sea and along the Jordan." But the men who had gone up with him said, "We can't attack those people; they are stronger than we are." And they spread among the Israelites a bad report about the land they had explored. They said, "The land we explored devours those living in it. All the people we saw there are of great size. We saw the Nephilim there (the descendants of Anak come from the*

71

Nephilim). We seemed like grasshoppers in our own eyes, and we looked the same to them."(Numbers 13:27-29 NIV)

Summary of the majority report as itemized below was astonishingly embarrassing and paradoxically perplexing:

1. The land flows with milk and honey - real confirmation of the surplus opportunities in the land. This proves that God's word is true and that Moses was not deceiving them by creating a rosy picture of non existent land supposedly made by a far and distant God.

2. We saw giants in the land –fact that there are threats and challenges in any given endeavour of life. Your case will not be different but the important thing is that ***every battle is winnable.***

3. The cities are fortified and the land devours its inhabitants and that the inhabitants are stronger than us. We are misfits, grasshoppers and no match to the inhabitants of the land. Comparatively they said we are not and cannot be better than any one else. They allowed fear, inferiority complex, self defeatism and wasp vision of insurmountable task to obsess the minds of the people. ***You will hardly win life's battles if the picture in your mind is that of defeat.***

4. We are not able to possess the land because God is not able to do what he said He would do – out of alignment with the plan of God for them thus invoking self destructive judgment.

What they saw in their minds was what they got. What they confessed was what they possessed. They all ended like grasshoppers with their carcasses littered in the wilderness along with those that believed this evil though majority report.

Minority Report (17%)

"Then Caleb silenced the people before Moses and said, "We should go up and take possession of the land, for we can certainly do it." (Number 13:30 NIV)

1. We are well able to overcome the land – winning mentality; I can do attitude. God-like attribute.

2. The enemies are pieces of bread for us –concentrate on opportunities and down play problems. This will release energy to push ahead.

3. God delights in us so He will give us the land –reliance on God is inevitable if you must win.

Could this be why the poor in the land out number the rich even today?

> *"Joshua son of Nun and Caleb son of Jephunneh, who were among those who had explored the land, tore their clothes and said to the entire Israelite assembly, "The land we passed through and explored is exceedingly good. If the LORD is pleased with us, he will lead us into that land, a land flowing with milk and honey, and will give it to us. Only do not rebel against the LORD. And do not be afraid of the people of the land, because we will swallow them up. Their protection is gone, but the LORD is with us. Do not be afraid of them." (Number 14:6-9 NIV)*

The slavery mentality the children of Israel had in Egypt affected their psyche and they saw themselves inferior to every one. They paid heavily for this flawed vision. Do not allow hopelessness and visionlessness to destroy you. It was only two among the twelve leaders that won on the inside that saw the real manifestation of the victory. What you see and think of yourself is important. *Are you having a twisted vision of your self? This is the time to straighten up your vision. If not you will end up being what God never intend for you.*

All Is By Choice

You are a product of choice. If for example your father chose not to marry your mother, there would have been no you. And if at the time you were conceived, they chose to be at daggers-end and refuse to meet, there would have been no you. If your father equally chose to marry another woman other than your mother, there would have been no you. It was by choice you came and you will also thrive or be destroyed by your choice.

If you decide today to walk out of poverty, all your faculties will respond in same direction. That simple you are asking? Yes. First decide within yourself that you will increase, be consistently focused and everything around you will be connected to looking for channels of increase.

Your thought will impact on the choice you make. Your choice equally will determine the actions you embark on and this will ultimately affect the results you obtain in life. Remember that you are liable for your actions.

Think and Not Worry

Many people misconstrue thinking to mean worry and vice versa. Thinking should be an integral part of our lives while worry should not be. We are choice making beings. Developing your thinking power is important in making good decisions. When you think, you are assessing situations, considering options, planning ahead and looking for solutions to any given problem or situation.

But when you worry, you are bothered about things you don't have control over and cannot change. Worry depreciates your health and dwarfs your ability to think right. It even affects your faith in God.

Jesus commands us not to worry.

> *"Therefore I tell you, do not worry about your life, what you will eat or drink; or about your body, what you will wear. Is not life more important than food, and the body more important than clothes? Look at the birds of the air; they do not sow or reap or store away in barns, and yet your heavenly Father feeds them. Are you not much more valuable than they? Who of you by worrying can add a single hour to his life? "And why do you worry about clothes? See how the lilies of the field grow. They do not labor or spin. Yet I tell you that not even Solomon in all his splendor was dressed like one of these. If that is how God clothes the grass of the field, which is here today and tomorrow is thrown into the fire,*

will he not much more clothe you, O you of little faith? So do not worry, saying, 'What shall we eat?' or 'What shall we drink?' or 'What shall we wear?' For the pagans run after all these things, and your heavenly Father knows that you need them. (Matthew 6:25-32 NIV)

Most people worry over what tomorrow holds, what to eat, what to wear and house to live. And each time things they have no control over are what they worry about. But God is saying *worry solves no problem.* So quit worrying and be involved in constructive and productive thinking. The day you stop thinking, you begin to diminish while you will start to increase the day you stop worrying.

Fill your mind with the word of God. Come off from mental slavery. Let the word of God shape your response to issues of life. It is well with you.

Chapter 7

SECURE YOUR FUTURE

Before Independence in 1960, the Nigerian economy was sustained largely by proceeds realized from the mother of all occupations -agriculture. Most families were basically agrarian using crude implements to carry out agricultural activities. The Government in a bid to increase revenues introduced various tax regimes. With the discovery of oil the economy received a boost with additional income source. Sadly, agriculture which was the main foreign exchange earner before discovery of oil in commercial quantity has been abandoned. In the case of Nigeria, it was adding one income line and removing one. So we cannot truly claim to have diversified income channels as a nation. That is why the country is limping. The industrial base is weak. Power is epileptic and unsustainable. Today in this country people that are largely dependent on agriculture especially using crude implements are not measuring up. And many that are solely dependent on single source of income cannot truly claim to be comfortable as a result of unfolding economic hardship. *The economic reality is that only few can survive comfortably on one or two streams of income.*

The Government is exploring other areas like solid minerals, tourism, etc, to broaden the income spectrum. This is on a countrywide perspective and how far the country will go on this expedition depends on the commitment of policy makers and implementers. Most companies are expanding their business frontiers by vying into ventures that make business sense either by backward or forward integrations or entering into entirely new terrains.

If the country and business concerns are intensifying efforts to diversify income base the individual should not do less. Developing or creating Multiple Streams of Income is imperative because when one source dries up there will be others to support. If income channel is one, when lost, this may take a long time to recover. Some people may not even recover at all from the fall.

You need portfolio of income streams. If you don't have streams of income it's time to create one. And if you have streams of income already add more because the future is not something that happens, it is something you make happen.

The point here is that one source of income was manageably enough in the yester years, two channels are not enough today and we need multiple channels of income for the volatile future.

The Bible has told us this unflinching truth but many are not listening. This central truth on multiple streams of income I repeat has been laid bare by God in the Bible. Prosperous people have realized this truth but sadly the poor are still far away from knowing this.

God's Perspective on Multiple Streams of Income

God in His wisdom formed different resources and carefully distributed them across the nations of the world. The basic aim for having different resources is to create different income channels for man. Individuals, organizations and nations that realized this and focus in expanding their income frontiers will always be stronger that those that are dependent on one source of income. God gave man charge to conquer the land, sea and air. Broadly speaking resources can be harnessed and distributed through these three areas.

Check out the following Scriptural verses:

> "The earth is the Lord's, and all its fullness, the world and those who dwell therein". (Psalm 24:1 NKJV)

> "For every beast of the forest is Mine, and the cattle on a thousand hills. I know all the birds of the mountains, and the wild beasts of the field are Mine. "If I were hungry, I would not tell you; for the world is Mine, and all its fullness." (Psalm 50:10-12 NKJV)

"The silver is Mine, and the gold is Mine,' says the LORD of hosts."

(Haggai 2:8NKJV)

The essence of God populating the earth with these natural resources is for man's growth and development. He could have chosen to make a-one-type resource world over. The world would have been unenjoyable. But the various resources provided by God provide a clear call to man to increase and diversify his income spectrum.

The Call That Many Have Refused to Heed

I implore you to carefully read the Biblical quotations below. We shall through them buttress God's clarion call to you to create multiple streams of income.

> *"Cast your bread upon the waters, for you will find it after many days. Give a serving to seven, and also to eight, for you do not know what evil will be on the earth. If the clouds are full of rain, they empty themselves upon the earth; and if a tree falls to the south or the north, in the place where the tree falls, there it shall lie. He who observes the wind will not sow, and he who regards the clouds will not reap. As you do not know what is the way of the wind, or how the bones grow in the womb of her who is with child, so you do not know the works of God who makes everything. In the morning sow your seed, and in the evening do not withhold your hand; for you do not know which will prosper, either this or that, or whether both alike will be good."*

(Ecclesiastes 11:1-6 NKJV)

Often and wrongly too, we limit interpretations of this portion of the Scriptures to giving, especially when there are calls for multiple givings in the Church. God's word is two edged sword, multi faceted and can minister to us in various areas of need provided we are open hearted to receive the undiluted and gracious word from Him.

Lets us define the key words and phrases contained in each verse of this Scripture quoted above before using same to drive home the call to increase your sources of income.

Cast- means throw or spread. This is a call to invest. To invest is to lay out money or capital in an enterprise with the expectation of profit (Verse 1). In the ancient days farmers cast their seeds across large expanse of plowed land. This is done with great expectation that those seeds will germinate, grow and provide fruits for harvest. So God is calling on you to spread your seeds into various investment outlets.

Your Bread – Your Bread here refers to unit or seed of investment. It is that seed you are holding right now. It might be small or big. No matter the size, it is seed for sowing. Don't waste it by spending all rather multiply it by sowing. Your bread could be eaten as food or sown as seed. If you are a salary earner, the salary is your bread but you can turn it to seed or you can even leave same as bread and consume all. Even when this verse is used to express giving, bread equally stands as seed. And that is why you are told to give expecting returns from the Lord.

Waters (same as Rivers of water in Psalm1: 3 and Isaiah 32:20) - Stand for different business ventures or various investment outlets. There are many investments channels out there with meaningful returns. You are to be selective in the kind of investment outlets to throw your bread to as you cannot be in all the waters at the same time. Bear in mind that there are waters of high and low currents. Trust God to lead you to still waters.

For You Will Find It After Many Days – Reaping/returns may not be immediate but will definitely come. There is time lag between the time of sowing and reaping, the time of investment and returns. The Bible is very clear that as the earth exits there will be seed time and harvest time. It is those that plow the land and sow their seeds will venture out to reap in times of harvest.

Paraphrasing verse 1 of Ecclesiastes chapter 11 we will have, *"**Invest your seeds in various investment outlets and you will definitely receive returns at the maturity period which is certain.**"*

Put some of your seeds in Savings, Fixed Deposit Account with the Bank or Retirement Savings Account. Invest in Insurance policies,

Real Estates and in Shares of companies with good fundamentals. Invest also in business enterprises. Diversify and never sink all your seeds in one line of venture.

Look at the timeless lessons contained in Verse 2:

> *"Give a serving to seven, and also to eight, for you do not know what evil will be on the earth."*

This verse urges you to add more additional income stream even if you have many already because a growing business may turn out failing tomorrow. The following salient points contained in this verse of Scripture are worth expressing:

1. Every business has its cycle or stages (growth, peak, decline). For example, a salaried worker who rose through the ranks, starts small, gets to peak of his career and is retired either voluntarily or forcefully. As he is moving up, the income increases through pay raise but as soon as he retires the income shrinks. If he is pensionable the monthly wages will turn out to be a fraction of what was paid when in full employment. And if not pensionable and without gratuity and preparations then life begins afresh on a rougher streak. And things may not be the same any more.

2. All businesses do not have the same cycle. Each stage on the cycle has its challenges that demands comprehensive and not wishy-washy attention.

3. For different businesses, there are different seasons for returns *(...that bringeth forth his fruit in his season, Psalm 1:3)*. You need to have some that will yield fruits in dry season and others in rainy season and if you have an all weather fruity investment the better for you.

4. Multiple Streams of Income (MSI) guarantee maintenance or sustenance of a given standard of living *(...his leaf also shall not wither, Psalm 1:3)*. The likelihood of all sources of your income drying up at the same time like the case of Job might be one in a million so move on

to create the hedge against declining from your present level of comfort by building multiple income streams steadily.

5. More settled to think, plan and invest *(…and whatsoever he doeth shall prosper, Psalm 1:3).* With multiple streams of income you are bound to be creative and not monotonous in devising new methods to keep increasing your income base.

In Verse 3 the risk factors in investment, certainty of returns and futility associated with failure to invest are addressed.

"If the clouds are full of rain, they empty themselves upon the earth; and if a tree falls to the south or the north, in the place where the tree falls, there it shall lie."

The verse stresses the following points:

1. Clouds signify different risk elements that abound in life and business ventures. They also symbolize unknown tomorrow, fears, haziness and inability to predict with absolute certainty the exact return from any given investment.

2. Every business has its risk elements. All businesses don't have the same risk elements. Fear of losses and of the unknown can stop you from investing and if you don't invest there will be no returns.

3. That all cloudy weathers do not end up producing rain calls for thorough risk analysis in investing purposes. Take calculated risks.

4. Rain emptying on the earth confirms certainty of returns for every risk taken. It is better stepping out boldly and taking risk than sitting down timidly feigning safety while doing nothing.

5. Bread eaten up and not put to investment uses, yields nothing, depreciates in value just like a cut tree lying dead on the ground being eaten by termites. The usefulness wanes with time.

Verse 4:

"He who observes the wind will not sow, and he who regards the clouds will not reap."

1. There are conditions, circumstances or factors that if observed or focused upon will discourage and militate against your investments and returns.

2. This verse urges that even when you don't feel like sowing, sow anyway.

3. When the investment climate and predictions don't support investing, invest anyway. ***The sane thing to do when you feel the weather does not support sowing is to keep sowing.*** Isaac was instructed to sow when the drought was all over the land. It never made business sense to do so. But he did and the rewards attracted attention from all and sundry.

Verse 5 underlines the God factor in your investment decisions.

"As you do not know what is the way of the wind, or how the bones grow in the womb of her who is with child, so you do not know the works of God who makes everything."

1. Begin and end your investment decisions or ventures with God. He is the one that gives the increase and protection to your investments.

2. There are uncertainties or forces that are outside your control which are subject to the authority of the Almighty God.

3. Do your own part and God will do His own part. Leaving God out in your investment decisions would ultimately be calamitous. You may have your way some times but if you persistently leave God out there is no guarantee you will make it to the finish line happily. This accounts why many are superfluously rich yet they are not happy. Some even end up having anticlimax committing suicide.

Verse 6 is a call not to be tired of sowing but to sow every time.

"In the morning sow your seed, and in the evening do not withhold your hand; for you do not know which will prosper, either this or that, or whether both alike will be good."

1. In the morning – When you are young, from the beginning of your career invest.
2. In the evening -When you are old, at retirement age invest.
3. When you feel like sowing, invest.
4. When you don't feel like sowing, invest.

Because (a) there is a possibility that your morning seeds will produce returns. (b)There are chances that your evening sowings will also produce results.

(c)There is also the possibility that both the morning and evening sowings will be fruitful.

From the explanations it is very clear and expedient to have multiple streams of income. Heed the call today and you will be happier thereafter that you did.

Jerusalem and Antioch Group of Churches

Let us throw our searchlights on the early Church with Head Quarters at Jerusalem and Antioch headed by Apostles Peter and Paul respectively taking a curious but comparative study on why the Church at Antioch was always supporting the Jerusalem branch with finances despite the fact that the Jerusalem Church being the first was supposed to lay for the Antioch Church.

It should be noted that the Church in Jerusalem started long before Apostle Paul was converted and by implication was supposed to lay down financially for the younger branch, but this was not to be.

We could adduce the reasons why the church at Jerusalem was always receiving aids from outside branches led by the church at Antioch as follows:

- ✓ Jerusalem Church Incorporated never knew nor ventured into the secrets of Multiple Streams of Income.
- ✓ The Antioch Church Incorporated knew and practiced Multiple Streams of Income.
- ✓ The Apostle Paul, the Head Pastor in charge of Gentile Group of Believers with Head Quarters at Antioch was both a Pastor and a practicing Tent Maker (Acts 18:3). Apostle Peter, Head Pastor of Orthodox Group of Believers with Head Quarters at Jerusalem was only a Pastor (although he was a successful business man who specialized in fisheries before he repented).

This explained why Paul was self sufficient not depending on any one for sustenance. So whether others were coming along with financial support or not one thing was basic, Paul was determined not to rely on this channel for sustenance. He could boldly say:

> *"You yourselves know that these hands of mine have supplied my own needs and the needs of my companions. In everything I did, I showed you that by this kind of hard work we must help the weak, remembering the words the Lord Jesus himself said: 'It is more blessed to give than to receive.'" (Acts 20:34-35 NIV).*

While Paul earned income through tent making and other financial support from the brethren, Peter's source of income was only that that came from support of the brotherhood.

- ✓ Jerusalem church depended on financial support from Antioch.

> *"During this time some prophets came down from Jerusalem to Antioch. One of them, named Agabus, stood up and through the Spirit predicted that a severe famine would spread over the entire Roman world. (This happened during the reign of Claudius.) The disciples, each according to his ability, decided to provide help for the brothers living in Judea. This they did, sending their gift to the elders by Barnabas and Saul." (Acts 11:27-30 NIV)*

> *"Now, however, I am on my way to Jerusalem in the service of the*

saints there. For Macedonia and Achaia were pleased to make a contribution for the poor among the saints in Jerusalem. They were pleased to do it, and indeed they owe it to them. For if the Gentiles have shared in the Jews' spiritual blessings, they owe it to the Jews to share with them their material blessings." (Roman 15:25-27 NIV)

While Jerusalem Group of Churches Incorporated are made up of Jerusalem and Samarian churches, Antioch Group of churches were made up of various country churches and house fellowships listed below: Romans, Corinthians, Ephesians, Galatians, Colossians, Philippians, Thessalonians, Miletus, Iconium, Island of Melita, Macedonian churches (2 Corinthians 8:1), Troas, Mitylene, Assos, Chios, Derbe, Lystra, Thytira, Phrygia, etc. House Fellowships include but not limited to Stephanas House fellowship (1 Corinthians 16:15-17), Aquilla & Pricila House Fellowship, Philemon, Titus, Onesiphous, etc.

2 Corinthians Chapters 8 and 9 exemplify how the Head Quarter Church at Antioch did raise funds to support the Church in Jerusalem.

You cannot be wrong in increasing your channels of income. God for sure is our source but His blessings come through various distribution channels. Key into this and explore into various channels of income and you shall be free from wretchedness and embarrassment.

Chapter 8

DEVELOPING FINANCIAL INTELLIGENCE

As this book was in writing I had a ride with two Navy officers one morning as I was going to my office. One was groaning bitterly that she would have retired in two thousand and seven after putting twenty five years in the service, but had to stay back when she found out that she had no retirement savings and investments. According to her, life in the last twenty five years has been living from pay cheque to pay cheque. She confessed in pains, bitterness and regrets that she never saw reasons to create additional sources of income through her regular monthly incomes over the years. Though investing in shares of companies she confessed was introduced to her several years back she only started to invest in shares though in small and no consistent manner few years back. But the good news for her was that she has become wiser now and has begun diversifying her investment (income) spectrum no matter how small. As the banters of discussions continued one could observe her colleague who obviously was pricked and literally disturbed by the discussions having no other sources of income but kept consoling herself that she will soon start diversifying her income channels. But what she did not know was that by postponing her investment decisions she was only eating up her tomorrow today. ***Don't eat up your tomorrow today through deferment or procrastinations of investment decisions.***

Imagine someone had worked for twenty five years in a job she never owned and yet there were no savings to show for it and the other one who's still dependent on the salary which could be stopped at any time is still procrastinating building a financial storehouse for tomorrow. This is catastrophic!

This is the kind of rat race that many people are in today; living from hand to mouth. These people depend solely on one source of income and not maximizing the use of it to better their tomorrow. *In fact if the truth must be told the pay day is usually the saddest day for many average salaried workers.* Reason is very simple – basically because the salary is hardly enough to meet all the needs lined up. And so what comes in is used to solve some of the immediate and at times not too pressing problems, while other problems are deferred till next month and many other problems are added before the next pay cheque. And this cycle continues month in and out and year in and out. Consequently, there is no provision for any savings and investments and by extension no improvement of financial well being.

In two thousand and eight the economic meltdown that started in United States of America courtesy of the sub prime mortgage loan, financial recklessness, greed and unbridled risk taking by most financial practitioners spread across the continents of the world. Many renowned companies in USA collapsed with the Government stepping in to bail out some key companies and banks to avoid systemic collapse of the financial system. Capital markets world over received serious shocking knocks.

The Nigeria Capital Market plummeted with investors losing billions of naira worth of investments. Most of the investments in the capital market were loans borrowed from banks that have turned to be toxic assets. The ripple effect of these economic meltdown was dwindling fortunes for individuals and companies and many able bodied workers were laid off due to no fault of theirs but the economic meltdown that started in a country far away which spiraled across the globe due the interdependence of world economies.

About ten banks in Nigeria due to over exposure to the capital market and oil sector and poor credit management had their capital eroded and became illiquid. This led to interventions by regulatory authorities to restore stability and confidence. With the shake up in the banking sector in Nigeria many qualified bank workers were sacked because of dwindling company fortunes. Many of the sacked workers never planned for this but the reality on ground is that the monthly pay cheque is no more. For those who saw this coming and took preemptive steps to prepare for tomorrow, this development will not be a total surprise and set back but an opportunity to try something else for them selves. But great number of the people who never prepared for this early and unexpected severance from their works will be devastated only blaming their management for picking and sacking them.

The truth is that once you are involved in paid employment you can go voluntarily or involuntarily. This is s secret that few discover on time and prepare for the inevitable. So start to prepare for your future enjoyment the day you gain employment by taking a well defined financial plan to build up wealth for tomorrow.

At the beginning of two thousand and three, I said I was going to walk out of financial subsistence into financial abundance by the end of that year. This may sound vague or ambiguous of a goal to many. But I have an idea of what I wanted. I started by giving several definitions to financial subsistence as "being controlled by your finances instead of being in charge of your finances; struggling to get along financially; agitated, being angered and having palpitating heartbeats when confronted with genuine and unavoidable financial concerns; dependence on only one source of income that is simply not enough to meet basic needs not to mention involvements in wealth replicating ventures." Not minding how broad and not too defined this noble target was nothing materially changed as long as I kept with the old habit of living from hand to mouth. Things only started to change when I took genuine practical and sustained steps (wishes alone and resolutions were hardly enough) to improve my financial lot.

I work with one of the first class banks in Nigeria. As bankers we tend to educate others on financial intelligence but most of us have poor financial habits and thus end up equipping others for a life of plenty while running around in cycles. Equally as bankers many times we live surreal lives (make believe kind of) because we are sure the staggering salary will come at the end of every month. Because every one is rushing to live in the coziest part of town, it doesn't matter even if you have to take your salary upfront just to belong. Don't get me wrong I am not against living in the best of places in town if your income can conveniently support that after all what is the part definition of comfort that money confers if you cannot enjoy out of it. But what is the sense in dashing landlord money every year because you want to be said to be living in a particular area of town when you can buy land somewhere else in town and erect your own building thus freeing yourself from being a tenant and the burden associated with it?

As bankers we literally work twenty four seven (slaves by choice) and hardly have the time to go for personal shopping. Thus those items we would have gone to purchase in the market places are brought right to us in the offices and we are urged to buy and give post dated cheques. We very often fall to this. Many of those items are sold to us more often than none three or more times their prices in the open market. There is no wisdom in continuing with this practice when you can get the items of purchase outside your office cheaper.

No matter your job, if asked to stop work today do you have any savings to keep going at least for the next three months without being a burden to someone else?

I sat back and checked the many millions that have passed through my hands since I started my banking career years back. Until then I never knew that I was a millionaire but who could not account for what has been happening to greater part of the millions.

I made a list of how my finances were applied. And I found out that I was spending on all expense heads ranging from fuel, travels, cars and car maintenance, cloths, feeding, rent, medical bills, electricity and telephone bills, school fees, offerings, tithe, charity, etc, but surprisingly I had no real savings. In fact savings was always postponed to the next month which never came. I found out that I was only enriching others by spending or wasting my income on things I came to call "expendables" and not on "dependables".

"Expendables" are those expense heads that take out from your income with no replicating effects. These constitute several holes in your income purse. While "dependables" are sources that replicate your income. They are such outlets that constitute channels for income growth. Thus I decided to deliberately reduce my spending on the expendables while increasing the dependables.

To keep spending on the expendables and build not the dependables is to be submerged deeper into the financial quagmire of poverty. Put in other words, to do nothing about the expendables is to keep living in financial embarrassments, intimidation and fear of tomorrow.

In a way I decided to be scientific with my spending, thus making the following decisions:

1. Save a little every month regardless of the pressures as there will always be financial pressures and the tendency is that *if you cannot save a kobo out of your ten naira today you may not be able to save ten naira out of your hundred naira tomorrow.*

2. Write out your needs for next month before the month's salary comes in and then prioritize. From the list, eliminate those that must be eliminated and defer those to be deferred. This to some might be cumbersome and to others a very simple exercise but in all this needs discipline to implement.

3. Have a financial plan and then stick to it. When expecting any income, plan ahead on what to do before the money comes in. When you are not too clear on what to do resist the pressure to spend now and plan latter. Rather warehouse the money until you can think straight and clear on what to do.

4. Don't spend on any item unless it adds value or solves a problem or meets a need.

5. Never spend to impress or spend impulsively.

6. Run away from the neck breaking yoke of buy today and pay later. It's never cheaper unless the value created far outweighs the cost.

7. Be conversant with prices and always go to where you will get same value at a lesser price.

8. Increase your income earning capacity. Seek how to increase your financial sources while at the same time reduce income leakages? What possible things can you do now that can generate additional incomes that you are not doing presently? What things are you doing which constitute leakages to your finances that must be stopped? These are the waste factors. Identify and eliminate them.

9. Who are your friends? What is the composition of your present friends? Are they all spiritual, social, family, or financial friends? Are these friends helping you to climb up, sink deep down or stand still? Do you need to expand the spectrum of friends? What advantage will this confer to you?

10. What are you doing to support the next person?

The test case is not in having financial strategic actions but in putting them to work. What will make the difference in your finances is not in hearing or reading these financial action plans but to what use you put them.

Some of these points and others will be expatiated in the remaining part of the chapter.

1.   Save A Certain Percentage Of Your Income

The syndrome of consuming all earnings that come in and then start to wait for the next pay day is a dangerous development or habit that must be expunged from your life style if you hope to break free from poverty to prosperity. An old axiom says that a little drop of water makes a mighty ocean. When you consume all your income, you are both eating the seed and the bread and there will be nothing to sow for tomorrow's harvest. No matter the pressures endeavor to set aside a certain portion of your income on monthly or regular basis. Some financial experts call this pay yourself first. For several years I was paying others but never paid myself first. But I know better now.

Save because life is full of ups and downs. There will always be rainy and dry seasons. There will also be years of plenty and years of famine. These eventualities of life are certain and cannot be changed by you but you can better prepare for famine and dry periods so as not to be consumed or suffer terribly. Apart from saving for precautionary reasons, economists tell us that you invest out of your savings. Thus without savings there will be no investments and no investments means no yields. Remember that when the unexpected happens in life you are expected to draw out of your savings to give the problem a frontal charge.

God enjoins us to save out of our income. This was illustrated in the advice given to Pharoah of Egypt by Joseph.

> *"Let Pharaoh do this, and let him appoint officers over the land, to collect one-fifth of the produce of the land of Egypt in the seven plentiful years." (Genesis 41:34 NKJV)*

Joseph advised Pharoah to save twenty percent of the produce of Egypt in the seven plenteous years. They were consistent with the savings and the reserve was sufficient to sustain the whole of Egypt and Canaan in the subsequent seven years of famine. What would have happened if Joseph's advice to save out of the plenty of Egypt was not heeded by Pharoah? The consequence is better imagined.

Any one that saves out of his earnings is called a wise man while any that spends all is called a squanderer and foolish. This is exactly what God said in *Proverbs 21:20*.

> *"There is desirable treasure, and oil in the dwelling of the wise, but a foolish man squanders it." (NKJV)*

2.   Invest Out Of Your Increase

There are tendencies that as your incomes are rising your expenses will be stepping up to match the incomes. Every promotion comes with salary raise but as you receive the increase set aside most of the additional income for investment purposes. It is wrong to step up your expenditures just as your income is increasing. It is better that your income is rising at a higher rate than your expenses are growing. **You cannot increase if you are in the habit of eating every money that comes your way.**

3.   Eliminate The Waste Factors

God owns the heavens and the earth. He could afford to be extravagant and wasteful; yet He is not. He laid a perfect example for us to follow when he fed the four and five thousand people with two and five loaves of bread respectively. Twelve and seven baskets of bread were gathered respectively and not wasted.

Many are poor not because they have not had a lot of income to set them apart but because most of those incomes are spent on waste factors that only contributed to their financial predicament.

I know some one that drinks a bottle of soft drink each time she eats any meal. She is so used to taking this pure carbonated water such that without it no food. This high consumption of sugar culminating to obvious addiction to me only increases the chance of being diabetic. At the time of this writing a bottle of soft drink is ₦50 (fifty naira). That means ₦150 (one hundred and fifty naira) per day and ₦54, 750 (fifty four thousand seven hundred and fifty naira) for a year. In ten years time she would have taken ₦547, 500 (fifty four thousand seven hundred and fifty naira) worth of sugar. What a record! Wouldn't the story be different if this money was set on annuity plan? The little drops per day from her wallet may not make sense but when aggregated, the impact is really much.

When you spend on expendables and not on "dependables" you are living wasted and are destroying your capacity to create wealth. The expendables are those items you can afford to do without which you are inextricably attached to. They are not really necessities; is not really that you cannot do without them but you keep them because of old habits and they constitute holes in your wealth wallet.

4.   Have Friends Across Board

> "*As iron sharpens iron, so a man sharpens the countenance of his friend.*" *(Proverbs 27:17 NKJV)*

Have friends among the rich. Have friends also among the poor. Your rich friends will be companions while your poor friends will inspire you to work harder and smarter. Note that there are problems that only your rich friends could solve for you and same goes for your poor friends. So you need both of them.

Jesus Christ of Nazareth the Saviour of the world had friends among the poor and among the rich and the two groups played different roles in His ministry. Jesus was friend to Lazarus, Mary and Martha. Women like Salome, Magdalene and a host of others ministered to the needs of Jesus. Among the rich and influential were Nichodemus, Joseph of Arimathea in whose tomb Jesus was buried was among the high and mighty in Jesus' day. In fact Joseph had the ear of Pilate such that he went in to him requesting the body of Jesus for burial.

> *"Joseph of Arimathea, a prominent member of the Council, who was himself waiting for the kingdom of God, went boldly to Pilate and asked for Jesus' body. Pilate was surprised to hear that he was already dead. Summoning the centurion, he asked him if Jesus had already died. When he learned from the centurion that it was so, he gave the body to Joseph. So Joseph bought some linen cloth, took down the body, wrapped it in the linen, and placed it in a tomb cut out of rock. Then he rolled a stone against the entrance of the tomb."*
> *(Mark 15:42-46 NIV)*

I don't think the request would have been granted if it was Peter or any of the other disciples that went to Pilate to request for the body of Christ for burial. Or what do you think? It has to be some one in the corridor of powers. That person was Joseph of Arimathea, a prominent member in the governing council. He boldly walked up to Pilate and placed a demand for Jesus' body and his demand was granted.

When Jesus had the Lord's Supper with the disciples, he sent the disciples to the house of a rich man to prepare the dinner. He did not send them to the house of any poor man for this purpose.

> *"Jesus sent Peter and John, saying, "Go and make preparations for us to eat the Passover." Where do you want us to prepare for it?" they asked. He replied, "As you enter the city, a man carrying a jar of water will meet you. Follow him to the house that he enters, and say to the owner of the house, 'The Teacher asks: Where is the guest*

room, where I may eat the Passover with my disciples?' He will show you a large upper room, all furnished. Make preparations there." They left and found things just as Jesus had told them. So they prepared the Passover.

(Luke 22:8-13 NIV)

This unknown host had a storey building with large guest room that was lavishly furnished to accommodate Jesus and the disciples for this all important last supper. This man couldn't have been a poor man to have this in those days.

Jesus ministered both to the poor and the rich. Your friends should equally cut across the rich and the poor.

5.   Start Small and Now

God will multiple your "something" no matter how small and not your "nothing".

God specializes in multiplying small things to big things. That's why He said don't despise the days of small beginning. The seed of miracle for your increase is not in that big thing you are wishing to have but in the small thing you have already. I have taken a little time to look into the Bible and have not seen any portion where it is written that God will bless your hand(s). God only blesses the works of your hands. In the days of Elijah the widow of Zeraphath and the son received a miracle of increase from the Lord out of the little flour she had. Out of a little oil the late prophet's wife in the days of Elisha received overflowing miracle that enabled her pay off the debts incurred by the late husband and had plenty thereafter. Jesus fed five and four thousand people with two and three loaves of bread respectively. Start with the small you have and believe God for increase.

6.   Be Customer Orientated

Money doesn't grow on trees. You find them in pockets of men and women. Your relationship with others is very paramount and to a great extent determines how far you will go. Be customer friendly. The money you need will not fall from heaven. The Angels will not come to your office to patronize you. The money will come through human channels – the customers. When your customers are satisfied with your service delivery, they make repeated purchases and possibly do a referral on your company. More satisfied customers will translate to more income growth. Many people make the mistake of thinking that they are in business just to make money. This wrong focus has ruined many businesses. Because they are in business to make money the customer that brings the money is secondary. If you open your office and there are no customers coming in, you will end up making no money and closing shop. So you are in business to serve the people that bring the money –the customer. Focus on the customer. Satisfy their needs and the money will keep coming in.

> *"Be sure you know the condition of your flocks, give careful attention to your herds; for riches do not endure forever, and a crown is not secure for all generations." (Proverb 27:23-25 NIV)*

If you are not careful of what constitutes money you will lose same.

7. Give Back to Society

You were not created for self. You were made to serve God and others. All around you abound cries for a lending hand. Your kind help can get somebody running again. It may save a life that may make a difference in the land tomorrow. Individuals that heed to the cries of the needy will attract God's attention and in times of trouble will not be destitute. The Scriptures says, *"bear ye one another's burdens and so fulfill the law of Christ" (Galatians 6:2)*. The quality of life you live is not necessarily determined by the volume of money you have but the number of lives you are able and willing to impact positively. You are not a success yet until you help some one else to succeed.

8. Don't be Lazy

Life does not deal favourably with the lazy. Laziness domesticates complacency and procrastination. And these are potent forces that can cripple and paralyze one's energy to overcome. The lazy has all desires and no actions and never realizes potentials. Don't defer till tomorrow what you can do today. Do whatever your hand finds to do now. The Lord in Proverbs chapter six instructs us to go to the ant and learn. The ants are small in size but big in intelligence. They know the reality of their weakness; the agility of their strength; possess the character to overcome threats and knack in discovering and realizing opportunities. With no leader to head the team ants move in colony and fight en mass against any predator. *They gather their food in the dry times against the rainy days and are always working. Jesus says my Father is working till now therefore I have to work. Why allow laziness to destroy you? Get up and get to work.*

Importantly, don't be lazy mentally. This is the worst kind of laziness. You have enough mental capacity to generate ideas that could translate you from poverty to riches. Don't be big head and no brain! Put your brain to work. Think!

Chapter 9

BETTER SIDE OF LIFE

"When we were at Mount Sinai, the Lord our God said to us, 'You have stayed at this mountain long enough. It is time to break camp and move on." (Deuteronomy 1:6-7)

You have stayed a long time in the camp of poverty and rejection. Now is the time to get up and match tenaciously forward. The great news is that no matter how low you've sunk, no matter how hard your life has been so far and no matter how bad and silly you have been beaten by circumstances of life there is hope for rising. There is a better side of life awaiting you. *All the best of God is ahead for you.* Release your faith on Him, work and hope for nothing but the best and never give up. This is because no matter the depth of your failings there is a hand waiting to lift you up. The righteous falls seven times and rises up again. Don't stay down. That is not the place for you. The Lord is our eternal refuge and His mighty hands are underneath us. You never can sink so deep that God cannot bear you. You are in Him. Just decide now to head to the better side of life and back your decision with actions. Don't be static! God hates stagnation. Get moving.

The Lord expects us to move forward and make progress in life. He said to Israel you have been in this position for too long. Your season for change has come so move forward. You cannot be in same unrewarding position and expect to grow and be great in life.

Even if you feel you have covered great mileages in life yet no matter the height of your achievements, there is always the next level so don't be complacent. Keep moving up with contentment and fear of God. Don't be destroyed by pride and in the midst of your material increase do not abandon your worship and service to God.

Life is interesting and beautiful if lived on purpose and could be frustrating if lived otherwise. The purpose of God is for you to have a full life of good health, financial abundance and spiritual soundness. Work to transit from the down side to the upside of life. *Everyday challenges confronting you present steps for you to move up.* They may have been brought before you by the enemy to sink you but God is turning things around for your good. To get stuck in complaints and blame apportionment will only stiffen your ability to work out from poor side to rich side of life. Indeed this is counter productive. No complainer or grumbler makes it to the finishing line.

There is the poor side of life and there is also the rich side of life. Interestingly, you can cross from one side of the divide to the other. History is replete with cases of people that came down from grace pinnacle of riches to despicable and reproachful grass cum pit of poverty and dejection. They got to the peak and neglected the God of their rising thus they had to hit the deck. There are also pleasant and encouraging stories of many that defied their low beginning, jettisoned complacency, shamed critics, mockers and detractors alike, and against all odds decidedly journeyed though painstakingly to desirable and enviable haven of pleasurable riches. Your present condition and or predicament are not enough reason for you to end up disillusioned and tired of life. Better days are ahead of you. Dust yourself up and get moving again.

From the various allusions in previous chapters it is very clear that poverty is the condition of being without adequate food and money. It is retrogressive walk only synonymous to unfruitfulness and barrenness in any given area of venture. The poverty could be mental, spiritual, material, etc. If poverty is being without adequate food and money, to be rich could be said to mean to have adequate food and money. To be rich is to be prosperous, flourishing, wealthy, owning much, etc. It is progressive increase in material acquisitions. Wealth, peace with God and man to me sums up the word true riches.

Riches and poverty are two irreconcilable poles. These are two different sides of the coin of life. You cannot live in poverty and in riches simultaneously. One drives out the other.

In life everyone is on transition. It is either you are moving up or down. It is either you are rich or poor. It is equally either you are failing or succeeding. Remaining on one level no matter the side you are in is unpardonable and abhorrent. So keep moving! If you are on the rich side seek to be richer and if you are on the poor side seek to extricate your self from the shackles of poverty. Many have allowed their poor state to turn to cul-de-sac (an inescapable dead end). It doesn't have to be so. Thus, decide and be committed to join the league of emerging class who are appropriating God's provisions to be rich men and women. You need join this moving train because no matter how you put it, to be rich is far better than to be poor.

Your poor condition is not a thing of joy to God which cannot be changed through self pity. Seeking for sympathy in pitiable state of poverty rather than provide a breather compounds the intricate and tenuous condition. You must have an understanding of what it takes to improve your lot. How do you think God will feel if you stand in front of a congregation in the Church to give the following testimony: Brethren! Praise the Lord! In fact I am happy that I am very poor, destitute and wretched that I cannot afford food for my household. The landlord has driven us out from his house because I could not pay the rent in the last two years and we are squatting under the fly over bridge. Above all brethren, I am happy that my brilliant children have dropped out of school because I could not afford their school fees. Praise the Lord! I can hear you saying that this is not testimony but an express indictment. Yet many of us are complacently happy taking poverty as the best that God gives.

Jabez in the Scriptures was very poor but he detested that condition (1 Chronicles 4:9). He was born into sorrow and pains yet he was upbeat in life, had a great desire for change of status and never sat down in despondency, whining and distraught, blaming everyone rather than self for his poor state. He prayed and trusted God for lifting and it was recorded that he was more prosperous than all his brothers. The brothers of Jabez were happy with their life predicaments and they did not fare any better. But Jabez who began life as a pauper refused to end poor. Whoever dares wins!

The world is made up of infinite possibilities waiting for whosoever that dares to launch out into the deep. Nothing is impossible to him that believes. Those that try inevitably have testimonies while those that take what life brings only tell tales of frustration, rejection and disappointment. God expects you to increase in all ramifications of life. He said:

> *"I wish above all things that you prosper and be in health even as your soul prospers." (3 John 3)*

First you should have a growing spiritual relation with God. Second you should increase in material well being and third have the good health to enjoy your wealth.

Given that God has set you free spiritually if you have personal relationship with Jesus Christ, He is equally out to set you free economically. Categorically, your freedom from the hands of Satan is not complete if it's limited to spiritual liberation. What do you mean you may ask? After all if I die now and poor after receiving the gift of salvation from sin, I will go to heaven! Who told you that all poor people will go to heaven? Since when did becoming materially poor become a precondition to entering into God's kingdom?

Remember also you are not just saved to die and go to heaven. You have a divine mandate that must be executed. ***You are not to be earthly useless in order to be heavenly useful. Therefore you must be economically liberated.*** God's riches must be entrusted into your hands to fulfill part of your divine mandate.

God demonstrated this irrefutable truth when He pulled Israel out from Egypt. He not only judged Egyptian gods in the process of setting Israel free, He transferred the wealth of the Egyptians to Israel. How about that? Moses and the entire people of Israel refused to leave Egypt when Pharoah, the king of Egypt asked them to go away in abject penury. The favour of God brought Israel into great state of wealth. Four hundred and thirty years of slavery and poverty was wiped off by a single moment of God's favour. You need God's splash of favour!

Many of us have left physical Egypt and its reproaches yet the heart and soul are still attached there because the cattle and precious jewels are still locked up in Egypt. This explains why many are drawn back to Egypt easily. They easily backslide in their commitment to serve God though they may be attending religious services and observing oblations.

Moses walked up to Pharoah insistently and vehemently demanded for their material possessions. Did he succeed? Yes! He got what was his and after that never looked backed to Egypt.

> *"Then Pharaoh summoned Moses and said, "Go, worship the LORD. Even your women and children may go with you; only leave your flocks and herds behind."*
>
> *But Moses said, "You must allow us to have sacrifices and burnt offerings to present to the LORD our God. Our livestock too must go with us; not a hoof is to be left behind. We have to use some of them in worshiping the LORD our God, and until we get there we will not know what we are to use to worship the LORD."*
>
> *(Exodus 10:24–26 NIV)*

Moses said not even a hoof that belongs to any Israelite will be left in the hands of ungodly Egypt. God set Israel free both spiritually and financially. Spiritual freedom without economic freedom is not total freedom. Get this real knowledge and don't be twisted or limited in your thinking that you don't need economic freedom after you are spiritually liberated. Spiritual liberation as a matter of fact should usher in financial freedom!

> *"During the night Pharaoh summoned Moses and Aaron and said, "Up! Leave my people, you and the Israelites! Go, worship the LORD as you have requested. Take your flocks and herds, as you have said, and go. And also bless me." The Egyptians urged the people to hurry and leave the country. "For otherwise, "they said, "we will all die!" So the people took their dough before the yeast was added, and carried it on their shoulders in kneading troughs wrapped in clothing. The Israelites did as Moses instructed and asked the Egyptians for articles of silver and gold and for*

clothing. The LORD had made the Egyptians favorably disposed toward the people, and they gave them what they asked for; so they plundered the Egyptians." (Exodus 12:31-36 NIV)

The children of Israel acted in consonance with the instructions handed down by Moses -God's Liberation Minister and the result was overwhelmingly amazing. They got silver, gold and clothing -all the best that Egypt had on offer. Their status was significantly changed as a result of their insistence not to go away empty handed. You need to have knowledge and key in to God's instructions to be free from poverty.

Aside this awesome experience Israel entered into the harvest they never laboured for in the land of Canaan. God is taking you to a place of sweet harvest. Trust and keep moving forward in obedience.

"And they did eat of the old corn of the land on the morrow after the passover, unleavened cakes, and parched corn in the selfsame day. And the manna ceased on the morrow after they had eaten of the old corn of the land; neither had the children of Israel manna any more; but they did eat of the fruit of the land of Canaan that year." (Joshua 5:11-12 NIV)

God launched His people into super abundance because He is God of abundance and what He has is for the children. The children of Israel came into carefully caught out increase. God was in it and it was gratifyingly awesome.

The Lord God is God of prosperity and is taking you to the wealthy place. Just as the house of joy is better than the house of mourning so is the wealthy place better than the poverty place. Thus God is lifting you up to the place of your increase.

As we are coming to the conclusion of this book I want you to fully understand that prosperity is God's message. *Prosperity is not new message. And it is not the make up of some people or Churches. Prosperity is not equally money message. It is not a wishy-washy teaching of some religious zealots. It is the message of the Lord.* Yes, prosperity brings money because you need money to solve lots of problems. Make no mistake about this money is good. It is no evil but a great lubricant that assumes the character of the holder. When the devil pins you down to believe that money is evil then you've got a big problem on your hands. You must clear off every polarizing belief wired in your system or risk being derailed by it.

Do you know that even if you can pray, exercise your faith, confess, proclaim and prophesy, and can equally bind, loose and cast out demons, at the same time you need money in your pocket to tackle and solve money problems. You may be anointed but all the same you need money in your pocket because anointing without money could be frustrating. In fact anointing without money is equal to annoyance.

In any Church that you have only spiritual, pious and faith proclaiming people without money people who are God fearing something is definitely wrong somewhere with that congregation. That Church in essence is deficient and not balanced in faith and works and may not effectively fulfill the divine mandate of reaching the world with the gospel. In fact that Church is not the place to be as their belief in God is not total.

Christianity which is relationship with God through Jesus Christ is a total and comprehensive package that embodies freedom not only from sin but from sickness, poverty and death. So don't be prosperity averse. Don't be afraid to prosper because you cannot attract what you hate. Don't be afraid to prosper because your God is very rich. Many are poverty stricken that they think that prosperity is sin. Prosperity is a covenant birthright of any one that believes in Christ whether black or white, Jew or Gentile. If you have affinity with God, prosperity belongs to you. But you must believe and appropriate what God says about prosperity for this to be real.

Jesus has exchanged your poverty and misery for His riches thus you don't have to be poor any more. Go forward and prosper in Jesus name. Amen.

ABOUT THE AUTHOR

Mr. Philip Nkwocha is a consummate banker with well over twelve years banking experience; six of which has been in Management positions. He is presently managing one of the Lagos branches of a leading bank in Nigeria.

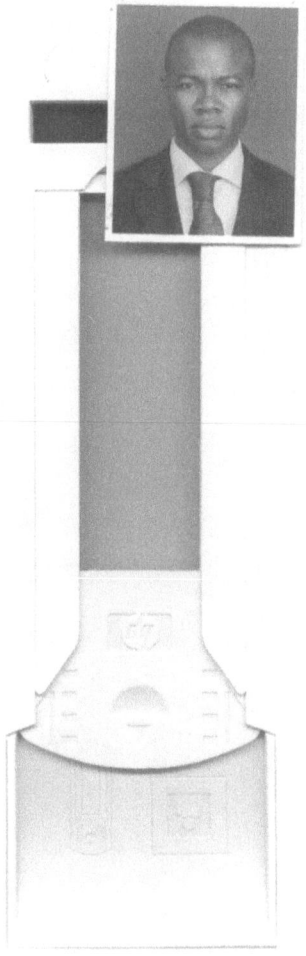

He is an Associate Member of the Chartered Institute of Bankers in addition to holding Masters Degree in Business Administration from ESUT Business School and Bachelors Degree in Finance & Banking from University of Port Harcourt, Nigeria.

Philip is a seasoned Bible Scholar, a Motivational Speaker, a Song Writer, a Financial Advisor and a Preacher of Righteousness who has featured in many churches and financial seminars and workshops in Nigeria. He is actively involved in services to God and humanity and is currently serving as a Deacon and Prayer Leader in Assemblies of God, Agboju, Lagos, Nigeria.

He got separated to the Lord through the home ministry of his father at the age of seven and believes in the totality of the Word of God. To him God is the source of all riches and the best of God belongs to those who serve and obey Him.

Philip is happily married with children.

www.ingramcontent.com/pod-product-compliance
Lightning Source LLC
Chambersburg PA
CBHW021545290526

45785CB00004BA/1515

9 781452 064307